Leida A. Willis, Ellen M. Wilsey

The Rumford Bread and Pastry Cook

Leida A. Willis, Ellen M. Wilsey

The Rumford Bread and Pastry Cook

ISBN/EAN: 9783337208622

Printed in Europe, USA, Canada, Australia, Japan

Cover: Foto ©Lupo / pixelio.de

More available books at **www.hansebooks.com**

Rumford

Differs from all other Baking Powders.

Rumford is a strictly pure phosphatic powder, and therefore is recommended by physicians as nutritious and healthful. Other powders are made of alum and cream tartar, neither of which are nutritious. Alum is condemned as unhealthful.

Rumford produces no bitter or other disagreeable taste in the food prepared with it, nor impairs the most delicate flavors. Many powders give a bitter or disagreeable "baking powder taste" to the food, and destroy the delicate flavoring.

Rumford produces Bread, Biscuit, Cake, etc., that will retain their fresh condition much longer than when any other powder is used.

Rumford is always full weight and uniform in strength. Cheap powders are generally short weight and vary greatly in strength.

Rumford is Sold at a Fair Price.

THE

Rumford

Bread and Pastry Cook.

Compiled by Miss LEIDA A. WILLIS,
Principal of the Baltimore Cooking School,

Assisted by Miss ELLEN M. WILSEY,
Teacher of Cookery, New York.

Rumford Yeast Powder

IS FOR SALE BY

M. Clark, 21 South Front Street, Philadelphia.
Rumford Chemical Works Branch, Cheapside & Water Sts., Baltimore,
Rumford Chemical Works Branch, 113 Commercial Street, Boston.
II. M. Anthony Co., 48 West Broadway, New York.
James II. Capers & Co., 8 South 14th Street, Richmond.
Rumford Chemical Works Branch, 6 Rush Street, Chicago.
G. J. Becht, 212 Eddy Street, San Francisco.

AND BY DEALERS GENERALLY.

Manufactured by the

Rumford Chemical Works, - Providence, R. I.

M. L. HORSFORD, Pres't. N. D. ARNOLD, Treas.

G-13 2-97

RUMFORD YEAST POWDER.

Is made of Horsford's Acid Phosphate, a pure bi-carbonate, and the finest starch. It is a strictly *pure* phosphatic powder, prepared by an improved process, and superior to all other baking preparations. It excels in baking strength and healthfulness, and produces biscuit, cakes, etc., that will retain their freshness longer than those prepared with ordinary baking powder, cream tartar or yeast.

Phosphates are found in all grains and meats used for food, and are essential to the healthy condition of the human body. Their lack causes ill health. Flour is largely deprived of its phosphates in bolting. This powder restores those nutritious and healthful elements. Its use is, on this account, recommended by physicians.

Read Carefully the following General Directions.

With the best ingredients, (which are always the cheapest,) careful measurements and good judgment in cooking, satisfactory results are sure to follow.

Milk is preferable to water for mixing, except for cake.

Do not use sour milk, or sour buttermilk with Rumford Yeast Powder.

Always sift flour before measuring it.

Less shortening is required when Rumford Yeast Powder is used than with the use of yeast, cream tartar or other baking powder.

Always use Pastry flour for cake, and Bread flour for bread, etc.

When butter is too hard to cream easily, heat the bowl slightly; never warm the butter.

Small ovens cool quickly; they should, therefore, be made several degrees hotter than a large oven, and the less the door is opened the better.

Do not attempt to bake bread and pastry together. Bread requires a prolonged, moderate heat; pastry the reverse.

Have a strong under-heat for Yeast Powder preparations, especially pastry.

3

INDEX TO RECIPES.

TABLE OF MEASURES.

1 teaspoonful salt	is 1 level teaspoonful.
1 teaspoonful sugar	" 1 rounded teaspoonful.
1 tablespoonful butter	" 1 rounded tablespoonful.
1 tablespoonful melted butter	" 1 level tablespoonful.
4 teaspoonfuls (liquid)	" 1 tablespoonful.
3 teaspoonfuls (dry)	" 1 tablespoonful.
2 tablespoonfuls (liquid)	" 1 fluid ounce.
4 tablespoonfuls (liquid)	" 1 wineglassful.
2 wineglassfuls	" 1 gill.
2 gills (½ pint)	" 1 cup.
2 cups	" 1 pint.
4 cups	" 1 quart.
1 cup butter (solid)	" ½ pound.
1 cup granulated sugar	" ½ pound.
2½ cups powdered sugar	" 1 pound.
4 cups of bread flour (sifted)	" 1 quart or 1 pound.
2 rounded tablespoonfuls flour	" 1 ounce.
1 rounded tablespoonful butter	" 1 ounce.
Butter size of an egg	" 2 ounces.

The World's Fair Award

Was Received by Rumford Yeast Powder.

4

RECIPES.

The Finest Cake in the World is made with Rumford Yeast Powder. See page 26.

BREADS.

White Bread. Sift together thoroughly 3 cups flour, 3 teaspoonfuls Rumford Yeast Powder, ½ to ¾ teaspoonful salt; add milk enough to make a dough just stiff enough to handle conveniently. Handle as little as possible with the hands, shape into loaf and place in a deep, buttered pan. Allow it to stand 5 minutes before placing in the oven. Bake slowly. Protect the loaf by placing a sheet of paper on top of it, buttering the side which comes next to the bread.

Whole Wheat Bread. Sift together thoroughly 3 cups whole wheat flour, 3 teaspoonfuls Rumford Yeast Powder, ½ to ¾ teaspoonful salt and 2 teaspoonfuls sugar. Add milk enough to make a dough just stiff enough to handle conveniently. Handle as little as possible with the hands, shape into a loaf and place in a deep, buttered pan. Allow it to stand 5 minutes before placing in the oven. Bake slowly and for a little longer than is customary to bake white bread. Protect the loaf by placing a sheet of paper on top of it, buttering the side which comes next to the bread.

NOTE:—Any dyspeptic may eat this bread without suffering from indigestion.

Graham Bread. Sift together thoroughly 2 cups graham flour, 1 cup sifted wheat flour, 3 teaspoonfuls Rumford Yeast Powder, 1 teaspoonful salt, 2 teaspoonfuls sugar. Pour over this sufficient milk to make a dough just stiff enough to handle conveniently, and proceed and bake same as White Bread.

Virginia Egg Bread. Scald ½ pint of yellow corn meal, making it moist, not wet. Add to this 1 tablespoonful shortening; when cool add 1 pint wheat flour, 1 teaspoonful salt and 1 teaspoonful sugar. To 2 well-beaten eggs, add 1½ cups milk; stir this into the dry ingredients. Beat well, and then add 2 heaping teaspoonfuls Rumford Yeast Powder. Bake in shallow pan about 45 minutes.

Rumford Brown Bread. Mix 1 cup yellow corn meal, 1 cup rye flour, ½ cup cold boiled rice, ½ teaspoonful salt, ½ cup molasses, 1½ cups milk; beat vigorously. Add ½ cup finely chopped dates, well floured, and 2 heaping teaspoonfuls Rumford Yeast Powder. Pour into a well-greased brown bread mould and steam 5 hours.

Boston Brown Bread. Mix together 2 cups yellow corn meal, 1 cup rye meal, ½ teaspoonful salt, 1 pint milk, ½ cup molasses and 2 heaping teaspoonfuls Rumford Yeast Powder. Pour the batter into a well-greased bread mould or tin pail and steam 4 or 5 hours; or bake in hot oven.

White Corn Bread. To 1 pint white corn meal, add 1 pint wheat flour and 1 teaspoonful salt. Rub into this 1 tablespoonful shortening; add 1 pint milk and beat well. Stir in 2 heaping teaspoonfuls Rumford Yeast Powder. Bake in shallow pans about 45 minutes.

Snow Drift Bread. Scald 1 cup white corn meal with 1 cup hot, boiled rice; add to this 1 tablespoonful shortening and when cool 1 cup wheat flour, 1 teaspoonful salt, 1 teaspoonful sugar, 1 cup milk. Beat well. Stir in 2 heaping teaspoonfuls Rumford Yeast Powder. Bake in shallow pan 40 minutes.

Breakfast Bread. To the well-beaten yolks of 4 eggs, add 4 tablespoonfuls flour, 1 tablespoonful melted butter, ½ teaspoonful salt, and enough milk to make a thick batter. Beat until smooth; then stir in gently, the whites of the eggs beaten to a stiff, dry froth, and 1 level teaspoonful Rumford Yeast Powder. Put 1 tablespoonful butter in a smooth frying-pan; when hot, turn in the batter, cover, and if the fire is *very* hot, place it on the back part of stove. When done, turn it out gently and serve with under side uppermost; or the batter may be poured into a well-greased baking pan, and baked in a *very* hot oven 15 minutes.

Thirds Bread. Mix thoroughly 2 cups yellow corn meal, 1 cup Graham flour, 1 of rye meal or flour, and 1 teaspoonful salt. Then add ½ cupful molasses, 1 cup milk and 2 of water. Stir into this, 2 heaping teaspoonfuls Rumford Yeast Powder. Pour into a well-greased mould or tin pail and steam 5 hours.

BISCUIT and ROLLS.

Rumford Biscuit. Sift together thoroughly, 1 quart flour, 1 teaspoonful salt and 2 heaping teaspoonfuls Rumford Yeast Powder. Rub in 1 large tablespoonful shortening. Mix quickly with sufficient milk or water to make a dough as soft as can be handled. Roll out 1 inch thick, cut with small biscuit cutter, place in heated biscuit pans and bake in a very quick oven for 20 minutes.

Drop Biscuit. Sift together thoroughly 1 quart flour, 1 teaspoonful salt. 2 heaping teaspoonfuls Rumford Yeast Powder. Mix quickly with sufficient cold water or milk to form a very soft dough. Drop tablespoonfuls of the dough into heated, greased pans, and bake in a very hot oven 10 minutes.

Whole Wheat Biscuit. Sift together thoroughly. 1 quart whole-wheat flour, 1 teaspoonful salt, 1 tablespoonful sugar, and 2 heaping teaspoonfuls Rumford Yeast Powder. Rub in 1 tablespoonful butter. Mix quickly with 1 cup cold water to a soft dough. Roll out 1 inch thick, cut with small biscuit cutter, place in well-greased, heated biscuit pans; brush with butter or milk, bake in a very quick oven 20 minutes.

Quick Cinnamon Biscuit. To 1 quart flour, add 1 teaspoonful salt and 2 heaping teaspoonfuls Rumford Yeast Powder. Sift three times. Rub in 1 large tablespoonful shortening. Mix rapidly with sufficient milk to make a dough soft enough to roll out without kneading. Turn out on well-floured board. Dredge with flour, roll quickly to a sheet 1 inch thick, spread lightly with butter, sprinkle with sugar, then a layer of currants, then cinnamon. Cut into long strips 2 inches wide, roll into biscuit, place in heated baking pans well greased, brush with white of egg, sprinkle with sugar and bake in a very quick oven 25 minutes. To be eaten while hot.

Biscuit without Shortening. Sift thoroughly together while dry, 1 quart flour, 2 teaspoonfuls Rumford Yeast Powder and 1 teaspoonful salt; then add sufficient milk to make a dough just stiff enough to handle conveniently. Handle the dough as little as possible. Have the oven hot before mixing, and always have the pans hot and greased. Cut out as many biscuit as possible before moulding again, as the extra handling makes the dough tough.

White Mountain Biscuit. Into 1 quart sifted flour, rub 1 tablespoonful butter; add 1 teaspoonful salt and 2 heaping teaspoonfuls Rumford Yeast Powder. Then to 1 cup cold mashed potato, add 1 cup milk or water; mix well with the flour. Knead lightly on board, roll out about 1 inch thick, cut with small round cutter and bake in quick oven about 20 minutes.

Egg Biscuit. Sift together thoroughly 1 quart flour, 1 teaspoonful salt, 2 heaping teaspoonfuls Rumford Yeast Powder. Then chop in 1 ounce butter. Beat 2 eggs light and add to ½ cup milk; mix the dough and bake same as Rumford Biscuit.

Gluten Biscuit. Beat 1 egg until light; add to it ½ pint milk. Sift together about 1½ pints gluten flour, 1 teaspoonful salt and 1 heaping teaspoonful Rumford Yeast Powder. Add to this gradually, the milk and egg; mix until smooth, form into small round biscuits and bake in quick oven.

Parker House Rolls. Mix 2 cups flour, 2 teaspoonfuls Rumford Yeast Powder, 2 teaspoonfuls sugar, ½ teaspoonful salt, sift twice; work in 2 tablespoonfuls butter with the tips of the fingers. Add gradually ⅔ cup milk, mixing until of the consistency of a soft dough. More or less is required according to quality of the flour. Toss on to a floured board and roll to ¼ inch in thickness, cut with a round or oval cutter, crease in the centre with the handle of a case knife, first dipped in flour. Brush one half with melted butter and fold over. Put in a pan ½ inch apart. Bake in a quick oven 15 minutes.

Fruit Rolls. Mix 2 cups flour, 2 teaspoonfuls Rumford Yeast Powder, ½ teaspoonful salt, sift twice; work in 2 tablespoonfuls butter with the tips of the fingers. Add gradually ⅔ cup milk, mixing until of the consistency of a soft dough. Toss on to a floured board and roll to ¼ inch in thickness. Brush over with melted butter. Sprinkle with ¼ cup stoned raisins and 2 tablespoonfuls citron, chopped fine, 2 tablespoonfuls sugar and ½ teaspoonful cinnamon. Roll up like a jelly roll. Cut into pieces ¾ inch in thickness. Bake in a quick oven 15 minutes.

Finger Rolls. Sift together 2 cups flour, ½ teaspoonful salt, 1 heaping teaspoonful Rumford Yeast Powder. Rub into this 1 teaspoonful butter; add water to make a soft dough. Form into rolls shape of fingers and bake in finger-roll pan in hot oven 20 minutes.

Cotta Rolls. To 1 quart sifted flour, add 1 teaspoonful salt; rub into this 1 tablespoonful shortening; then add 2 heaping teaspoonfuls Rumford Yeast Powder and enough milk to make a soft dough. Turn out on board and knead lightly; roll out about ½ inch thick; cut out with a large round cutter, brush over with butter, dredge with flour and fold in two. Bake in a hot oven about 15 minutes.

Egg Rolls. Beat without separating, 2 eggs, adding to them ½ cup milk. Sift 1 pint flour with ½ teaspoonful salt; rub into this ½ tablespoonful butter, and add 1 heaping teaspoonful Rumford Yeast Powder and the milk and egg. Form into small oblong rolls and bake.

Fairie's Bread. Sift together 2 cups whole-wheat flour, ½ teaspoonful salt, 1 rounded teaspoonful Rumford Yeast Powder. Beat to a cream 2 large tablespoonfuls butter and 2 large tablespoonfuls brown sugar; add 2 eggs well-beaten, 1 teaspoonful ginger, 1 teaspoonful cinnamon, a pinch of cloves and ½ cup milk. Quickly stir in the flour; mix well. Spread the batter very thin on baking sheets. Place in very moderate oven and bake a pale brown. Cut into squares as soon as done.

Salad Sticks. For these salad sticks use the recipe for Finger Rolls, making one-quarter the quantity. After the dough has been made, work in with the hand, the beaten white of 1 egg, 1 teaspoonful powdered sugar and 1 teaspoonful butter. When well mixed add more flour—enough to make the dough very stiff. Knead well, break off pieces size of a hickory-nut, wet palms of the hands with milk and roll out the dough about as thick as a lead pencil. Put in baking pan and bake in *cool* oven ½ hour. Should be brown and crisp.

Rumford Horns. To 1 quart sifted flour, add 1 teaspoonful salt, 2 heaping teaspoonfuls Rumford Yeast Powder and 1 tablespoonful sugar, into which rub thoroughly 1 tablespoonful butter. Then add about ½ pint milk. Mix well, turn out on board, roll out about ¼ of an inch thick. Cut into six-inch squares and cut across each square from corner to corner, making four three-cornered pieces of each square. Brush over top of each with butter and dredge lightly with flour. Roll up from large side, lay on baking-pan with pointed side uppermost, and bend round in shape of horse-shoe. Brush over top with egg, and bake in hot oven until a light brown.

GEMS and MUFFINS.

Rumford Corn Gems. Sift and scald sufficiently to just moisten, 2 cups white corn meal. Add while hot 1 level tablespoonful shortening. When cool, separate 2 eggs; beat yolks until light, add to meal with 1 cup milk; beat vigorously until smooth. Add 1 teaspoonful each, salt and sugar, before scalding the meal. Stir carefully into the batter, 1 heaping teaspoonful Rumford Yeast Powder and the whites of the eggs beaten stiff. Pour into well-greased gem pans and bake in a quick oven 30 minutes.

Rice Gems. To ½ cup cold boiled rice, add the well-beaten yolks of 3 eggs, 2 cups milk, 1 teaspoonful salt, 3 cups sifted flour and 1 tablespoonful melted butter. Beat vigorously until batter is perfectly smooth. Now add carefully 2 heaping teaspoonfuls Rumford Yeast Powder and whites of the eggs beaten stiff. Bake in hot gem pans in very quick oven.

Cold Oatmeal Gems. To 1 egg well-beaten, add 1 cup milk or water. Mix well 1 cup cold oatmeal, 1 cup wheat flour, ½ teaspoonful salt and 1 teaspoonful shortening. Add to this the milk and egg and 1 heaping teaspoonful Rumford Yeast Powder. Bake in moderate oven about 25 minutes.

Whole Wheat Gems. Separate 4 eggs; beat yolks very light. Add 2 cups milk, 2 tablespoonfuls brown sugar, 4 cups whole-wheat flour sifted with 1 teaspoonful salt; add 2 tablespoonfuls melted butter. Mix in carefully 2 heaping teaspoonfuls Rumford Yeast Powder and the whites of eggs beaten to a stiff froth. Fill well-greased, heated gem pans nearly full and bake in a quick oven 30 minutes.

Gluten Gems. Beat the yolks of 2 eggs; add to them 1 cup milk, 2 teaspoonfuls melted butter, ½ teaspoonful salt. Add to this, about 1½ cups gluten flour, 1 heaping teaspoonful Rumford Yeast Powder and the whites of the eggs beaten to a stiff froth. Bake in quick oven about 25 minutes.

Tip Tops. Separate 3 eggs; beat yolks slightly; then add gradually 2 cups *cold* water and beat briskly until light and foamy. Stir very carefully into 2 cups well-sifted flour, making a smooth batter; strain through a fine sieve. Add ¼ teaspoonful salt and 1 tablespoonful melted butter; mix well. Stir in 1 heaping teaspoonful Rumford Yeast Powder and whites of the eggs beaten to a stiff froth. Bake in hot gem pans.

Economy Gems. Beat 1 egg; add to it, 1 cup milk, 1 tablespoonful melted shortening, ½ teaspoonful salt, 2 teaspoonfuls sugar, 2 cups flour and 1 heaping teaspoonful Rumford Yeast Powder. Bake in hot oven about 20 minutes.

Whole Wheat Fruit Gems. To the well-beaten yolks of 3 eggs, add 1 cup milk, 1 tablespoonful melted shortening, ½ teaspoonful salt, 2 cups whole-wheat flour, and 1 heaping teaspoonful Rumford Yeast Powder. Stir in gently, the whites of eggs beaten to a stiff froth and 1 cupful chopped figs well floured. Bake in gem pans about 25 minutes.

Hominy Grits Muffins. To 2 eggs well-beaten, add 2 cups milk and 1 of water, 1 quart of flour into which 1 tablespoonful shortening has been rubbed, 1 teaspoonful salt, 2 heaping teaspoonfuls Rumford Yeast Powder and 1 cup cold boiled grits. Bake in muffin rings on hot griddle, or in gem pans in hot oven about 20 minutes.

Plain Muffins. To 1 pint milk, add the well-beaten yolks of 3 eggs and 2 tablespoonfuls melted butter. Sift together 3 cups flour, 1 teaspoonful salt and 2 teaspoonfuls Rumford Yeast Powder. Add to this gradually the milk and yolks of eggs; now stir in carefully the well-beaten whites, pour into greased muffin rings and bake on hot griddle or in gem pans in oven.

Rumford Muffins. Scald 1 cup white corn meal, making it moist, not wet. While hot, add 1 tablespoonful shortening. When cool, add 1 cup rye flour, 1 teaspoonful salt, 2 tablespoonfuls sugar, 2 rounded teaspoonfuls Rumford Yeast Powder and enough milk to make a batter that will drop from spoon.

Bake in well-greased muffin rings on a hot griddle, or in gem pans in oven.

Water Muffins.

To 1 pint water add 1 tablespoonful melted butter and 1 teaspoonful salt. Into 3 cups flour sift 2 rounded teaspoonfuls Rumford Yeast Powder. Mix with the water and melted butter, and bake in muffin rings or in gem pans in hot oven about 20 minutes.

Quick English Muffins.

Sift together twice, 1 quart flour, 1 teaspoonful salt, 2 heaping teaspoonfuls Rumford Yeast Powder. Mix quickly with 1 pint *cold* water into a *very* soft dough. Now add whites of 2 eggs beaten very stiff. Place flour in a saucer, drop in a piece of the dough, shape quickly into muffins, bake on a hot griddle; turn and brown on both sides.

Rye Muffins.

Separate 2 eggs; beat yolks until light; add 1½ cups milk. Sift together 1 cup rye meal, 1 cup flour, ½ teaspoonful salt and 1 tablespoonful brown sugar; add these to the liquid with 1 tablespoonful melted shortening. Beat briskly for a few minutes, then add 2 heaping teaspoonfuls Rumford Yeast Powder and the whites of the eggs beaten to a stiff froth. Bake in muffin rings on a hot griddle 20 minutes.

Breakfast Muffins.

To 2 cups flour, 1 tablespoonful sugar and ½ teaspoonful salt well sifted together, add 1½ cups milk and 1 tablespoonful melted butter; beat vigorously until perfectly smooth. Mix in carefully 2 rounded teaspoonfuls Rumford Yeast Powder. Bake in rings on a hot griddle 15 or 20 minutes; turn and brown on both sides.

Crumpets.

Made same as Breakfast Muffins, but baked in larger rings, and split open and toasted when eaten.

Harford Muffins.

Beat the yolks of 2 eggs slightly; add gradually 1½ cups cold water, beating vigorously until light and foamy. Sift 2 cups flour, 2 tablespoonfuls corn meal, 2 tablespoonfuls sugar and ½ teaspoonful salt together; add to the liquid with 1 tablespoonful melted butter. Then stir in 2 teaspoonfuls Rumford Yeast Powder and the whites of the eggs beaten to a stiff froth. Bake in muffin rings on hot griddle 15 or 20 minutes.

Farina Muffins.

To 1 cup hot farina mush, add 2 teaspoonfuls butter; when cool, beat the yolks of 3 eggs very light; add to them 2 cups milk, 3 cups flour, 1 teaspoonful salt, and farina. Beat well for 5 minutes; then add 2 heaping teaspoonfuls Rumford Yeast Powder and the whites of eggs beaten stiff. Bake in muffin rings in a very quick oven 25 minutes.

Rice Muffins. Sift together 2½ cups flour, ½ teaspoonful salt and 3 teaspoonfuls Rumford Yeast Powder. Add 1 cup boiled rice, working in with the tips of the fingers. Add gradually 1 cup milk, 1 egg well beaten, and ¼ cup melted butter. Butter muffin rings, place in a buttered pan; fill ⅔ full with the mixture. Bake in a moderate oven 25 to 30 minutes. The same mixture may be baked in gem pans.

Corn Muffins. Mix and sift 1 cup cornmeal, ¾ cup flour, 2 teaspoonfuls Rumford Yeast Powder, and 1 teaspoonful salt. Add gradually ¾ cup milk and ¼ cup molasses. Beat thoroughly. Add 1 egg well beaten and 1 tablespoonful melted butter. Bake in hot, buttered gem pans 25 minutes.

Berkshire Muffins. Scald 1 cup cornmeal with 1¼ cups hot milk. Let stand 5 minutes. Add 1 cup boiled rice, and 1 cup flour to which has been added 3 teaspoonfuls Rumford Yeast Powder, 1 teaspoonful salt and ¼ cup sugar. Add the yolks of 2 eggs beaten until thick, 1 tablespoonful melted butter and the well beaten whites of the eggs. Bake in hot, buttered gem pans 25 minutes.

Quaker Muffins. Turn 1 cup scalded milk on to ⅔ cup rolled oats; let stand 5 minutes. Add 1 teaspoonful salt, 3 tablespoonfuls sugar, and 1 tablespoonful melted butter. Sift in 1⅓ cups flour and 2 teaspoonfuls Rumford Yeast Powder; add 1 egg well beaten. Bake in hot, buttered gem pans 25 minutes.

Squash Muffins. Add 1 cup milk to ⅔ cup cooked squash. Add ¼ cup sugar and 1 egg, well beaten. Sift 1 teaspoonful salt and 3 teaspoonfuls Rumford Yeast Powder with 2¾ cups flour and add to the first mixture; add 1 tablespoonful melted butter. Beat thoroughly and bake in hot, buttered gem pans 25 minutes. If intended for luncheon or tea, ¼ teaspoonful of cinnamon, nutmeg or ginger may be added.

GRIDDLE CAKES.

Rumford Buckwheat Cakes. To 1 quart cold water add 1 teaspoonful salt, 3 cups pure buckwheat flour and ¾ cup white corn meal; beat until perfectly smooth, cover and let stand for a short time in a moderately warm place. When ready to use add 2 heaping teaspoonfuls Rumford Yeast Powder. Mix thoroughly; bake on a smoking-hot griddle. Serve at once with Honey or Grape Syrup. (*Never put molasses in buckwheat cakes, it makes them bitter.*)

Quick Batter Cakes. Beat slightly the yolks of 4 eggs; add gradually 3½ cups cold water; beat until light and foamy; sift together 1 quart flour, 8 tablespoonfuls corn meal and 1 teaspoonful salt; stir in the liquid and beat vigorously until smooth; add 2 tablespoonfuls melted butter and beat again; add 2 heaping teaspoonfuls Rumford Yeast Powder and whites of eggs beaten stiff; bake on hot griddle. Serve hot with butter and sugar.

Queen's Griddle Cakes.

One-and-one-half cups fine bread crumbs soaked in 3 cups milk until soft; add yolks of 2 eggs beaten light; stir this carefully into 2½ cups flour; add ½ teaspoonful salt, 3 teaspoonfuls sugar, little nutmeg, grated peel of 1 lemon and 1 tablespoonful melted butter; beat briskly for a few minutes, then add 2 heaping teaspoonfuls Rumford Yeast Powder and the whites of the eggs beaten stiff; bake on a hot griddle. *Small fruits may be added to this batter; they should be well floured.*

Rice Griddle Cakes.

Sift 3 cups flour with 1 teaspoonful salt into a bowl; beat yolks of 2 eggs light; add 2 cups milk and stir carefully into the flour; add 1 cup cold boiled rice and 1 tablespoonful melted butter; beat briskly a few minutes; add 2 heaping teaspoonfuls Rumford Yeast Powder and whites of the eggs beaten to a stiff froth. Bake on hot griddle.

Cold Oatmeal Griddle Cakes.

To the well-beaten yolks of 3 eggs add 2 cups milk, or milk and water mixed. 2 tablespoonfuls butter melted, 1 teaspoonful salt, 1 cup cold boiled oatmeal, 3 cups flour, and 2 heaping teaspoonfuls Rumford Yeast Powder. Stir in the whites of eggs beaten to a stiff froth, and bake on a hot, well-greased griddle.

Potato Griddle Cakes.

To 1 cup cold mashed potatoes add the yolks of 2 eggs well-beaten, 2 cups milk, 2 tablespoonfuls butter, melted, 1 teaspoonful salt, 3 cups flour, and 2 heaping teaspoonfuls Rumford Yeast Powder. Stir in carefully the whites of eggs beaten to a stiff froth, and bake on hot, well-greased griddle.

Rumford Griddle Cakes.

Soak ¼ cup bread-crumbs in 1 cup milk; then add 1 egg well-beaten, ½ teaspoonful salt, 1 rounded teaspoonful Rumford Yeast Powder and 1 cup flour; mix well. Bake on hot, well-greased griddle.

Indian Meal Griddle Cakes.

Scald 2 cups yellow Indian meal, making it moist, not wet. Add to it while hot 1 tablespoonful shortening. When cool add 1 cup flour, 1 teaspoonful salt, 2 eggs well-beaten, and add gradually 1 pint milk. Now stir in 2 heaping teaspoonfuls Rumford Yeast Powder. Bake on hot griddle.

CORN CAKES, PONE, SHORT CAKES, Etc.

Corn and Rice Cakes. Mix 1 cup white corn meal with 1 cup hot boiled rice. Add 1 tablespoonful butter, ½ teaspoonful salt, 2 rounded teaspoonfuls Rumford Yeast Powder, ½ cup sugar, 1 cup milk. Beat vigorously and bake in gem cake-pans in hot oven about 25 minutes.

Rumford Corn Cake. Beat 2 eggs, add to them 3 table-spoonfuls sugar, 1 pint milk, 1 teaspoonful salt, enough white corn meal or flour to make a soft batter. Then stir in 2 heap-ing teaspoonfuls Rumford Yeast Powder. Bake in shallow pan about 25 minutes.

Carolina Corn Cake. Pour over 2 cups white corn meal sufficient boiling water to scald, but not to make it wet; add to it while hot 1 tablespoonful shortening. When cold add 2 eggs well-beaten, 2 cups sweet milk, 1 teaspoonful salt, 1 cup corn flour and 2 heaping teaspoonfuls Rumford Yeast Powder. Pour into long shallow pans, and bake in a quick oven 45 minutes. When done cut into square blocks. The batter should be rather thick.

Johnny Cake. Sift together thoroughly 2 cups corn meal, 1 large tablespoonful flour, 1 teaspoonful salt, 1 tablespoonful sugar and 2 teaspoonfuls Rumford Yeast Powder. Rub 1 tablespoonful shortening into meal; then add 2 cups milk or water; mix into a smooth, firm batter; pour into shallow pans and bake in a quick oven 45 minutes. A few apples sliced very fine are an addition.

Southern Corn Custard. Scald 1 cup white corn meal with sufficient boiling water to make a thin batter; add 1 teaspoon-ful salt, and steam 1 hour; there should be 2 cups of thin mush when done. While hot add 1 tablespoonful shortening and 1 tablespoonful sugar. When cold add 1 cup milk, well-beaten yolks of 3 eggs and ¾ cup flour; beat to a smooth, firm bat-ter, then add 2 teaspoonfuls Rumford Yeast Powder and whites of eggs beaten stiff. Bake in shallow pans in a quick oven 25 minutes.

Corn Dodgers. Scald 3 cups white corn meal, making a stiff batter; add 1 tablespoonful shortening, 1 teaspoonful salt and 1 teaspoonful sugar; beat vigorously for a few minutes; add 2 well-beaten eggs and 2 teaspoonfuls Rumford Yeast Pow-der. Drop large spoonfuls in hot buttered pans, flatten on top with the spoon; the batter must not be thin enough to run. Bake in a very quick oven 15 minutes.

Hominy Grits Cakes. Sift together 2 cups flour and 1 tea-spoonful salt; add the well beaten yolks of 2 eggs, 1 cup milk and 1 tablespoonful melted butter; beat smooth; add 2 cups cold boiled hominy grits, and beat again; stir in carefully 2 heaping teaspoonfuls Rumford Yeast Powder and whites of the eggs beaten to a stiff froth. Half fill muffin rings on a hot griddle and bake in a quick oven 20 minutes.

Wheaton Scones. Sift together 2 cups whole-wheat flour; 1 cup flour, 1 teaspoonful salt; rub in 1 level tablespoonful shortening; add 2 eggs beaten very light, sufficient milk to make a very stiff batter, and 2 heaping teaspoonfuls Rumford Yeast Powder. Drop from a large spoon into a hot, well-greased pan and bake in a very quick oven 15 minutes. This dough can be made stiff enough to roll out and cut into triangles.

Little Indian Cakes. Scald 2 cups white corn meal; add to it 1 tablespoonful shortening, ½ cup sugar, ½ teaspoonful salt and enough milk or water to make a drop batter. Stir into this ½ cup raisins or dried currants and 2 rounded teaspoonfuls Rumford Yeast Powder. Drop on hot, well-greased bake-iron, or bake in very hot oven in biscuit-pan.

Orange Short Cake. Beat 1 egg; add to it 1 cup milk, ½ teaspoonful salt, 1 tablespoonful butter melted, 2 tablespoonfuls sugar. Sift into 2 cups flour 1 heaping teaspoonful Rumford Yeast Powder. Moisten this with the milk and egg; mix well; knead lightly on board and roll out, making 2 cakes, one a little thicker than the other. Place the thicker cake in a well-greased jelly-cake tin, spread with butter, place the thinner cake on top and bake in a hot oven about 20 minutes. Cut 2 or 3 oranges into dice, sprinkle with sugar and grated cocoanut. When the cakes are baked, separate them and while hot spread the lower layer with the orange mixture; cover with the other layer and spread the top with orange icing and whipped cream.

Orange Icing. To 4 tablespoonfuls powdered sugar add the grated yellow rind of ½ an orange, and enough juice to moisten it.

Apricot Short Cake. Make same as Orange Short Cake, using apricots slightly mashed and sprinkled with sugar to place between the layers. Spread the top with a meringue made from the white of 1 egg and 1 tablespoonful sugar, beaten until stiff.

Cream Short Cake. Sift together 3 times, 1 quart flour, 1 teaspoonful salt and 2 heaping teaspoonfuls Rumford Yeast Powder. Now see that your oven is hot; then moisten the flour with ½ pint rich cream and 1 gill milk, making a dough as soft as can be handled; knead lightly and quickly; roll out 1 inch thick, cut into small, round biscuits and bake in a quick oven 20 minutes.

Strawberry Short Cake. Sift 2 heaping teaspoonfuls Rumford Yeast Powder, and 1 teaspoonful salt with 1 quart flour. Rub in 2 ounces butter and moisten to a very soft dough with cold milk. Mix quickly and lightly; pat out into a large round cake 2 inches thick; place in a large, square baking-pan and bake in a very quick oven 20 minutes. While hot pull apart; spread both halves with good, sweet butter, not pressing but dropping it on with a knife; spread the lower half with a thick layer of slightly crushed, sugared strawberries; put on the top crust, dust with sugar, heap with sweetened, whipped cream, and garnish with a few large berries. Serve at once, and cut with a hot knife.

Virginia Pone. Scald 1 quart white corn meal, and while hot add to it 2 tablespoonfuls shortening and 1 teaspoonful salt. When cool add 1 pint milk and 2 heaping teaspoonfuls Rumford Yeast Powder. Mix well and bake in a well-greased, shallow baking-pan about 40 minutes.

WAFFLES, PANCAKES, Etc.

Waffles. Beat yolks of 3 eggs until light, with 1½ cups pulverized sugar; add 1 pint milk, 3 cups flour sifted with 2 level teaspoonfuls Rumford Yeast Powder, ½ teaspoonful salt, 1 ounce melted butter, and the whites of eggs beaten light. Mix carefully; pour batter into hot, well-greased waffle-irons, cover quickly, turn and brown both sides; bake 2 or 3 minutes. Dust with sugar when done.

Rumford Waffles. Beat the yolks of 2 eggs until very light; add to them 1 pint of milk, or milk and water mixed, 3 cups flour, into which has been rubbed 2 tablespoonfuls shortening, 1 teaspoonful salt and 2 rounded teaspoonfuls Rumford Yeast Powder. Now stir in carefully the whites of eggs beaten to a stiff froth. Grease the waffle-iron well and fill with the batter, close, turn quickly and bake until nice brown.

Corn-Flour Waffles. To the beaten yolks of 2 eggs, add 1 pint milk, or milk and water mixed, 3 cups corn flour, 1 teaspoonful salt, 1 tablespoonful melted shortening, 2 heaping teaspoonfuls Rumford Yeast Powder. Stir in carefully the whites of eggs well-beaten, and bake in a hot well-greased waffle-iron for about 2 minutes.

Rice Waffles. Beat the yolks of 2 eggs until light; add to them 1 cup cold boiled rice, 2 cups milk, 1 teaspoonful salt, 2 tablespoonfuls melted butter, 2 cups flour and 2 heaping teaspoonfuls Rumford Yeast Powder. Stir in carefully the well-beaten whites of eggs and bake in well-greased hot waffle-iron until a delicate brown.

Apple Pancakes. Sift together 1 pint flour, ½ teaspoonful salt and 1 rounded teaspoonful Rumford Yeast Powder, and add to it 1½ cups grated apple, and 1½ cups luke-warm water. Grease a small frying pan well and when hot pour in the batter; when brown on one side, turn and brown on the other; remove carefully from pan, spread with butter, sprinkle with sugar, roll, and serve while hot.

Potato Pancakes. To 1 cup cold mashed potato add ½ teaspoonful salt, 1 cup milk, the grated rind of ½ a lemon, 1 rounded teaspoonful Rumford Yeast powder, and enough flour to make a thin batter. Bake and serve the same as Apple Pancakes.

Fine Pancakes. Beat the yolks of 4 eggs with 2 tablespoonfuls sugar until very light; add 1 pint rich cream and a pinch of salt; stir this carefully into 4 large tablespoonfuls sifted flour, making a perfectly smooth batter; add ½ teaspoonful rose or orange-flower water, a little nutmeg, whites of eggs beaten stiff and 1 heaping teaspoonful Rumford Yeast Powder. Put 1 tablespoonful butter into a small, round skillet, place over the fire until it smokes, pour in enough batter to cover bottom of pan; brown, then turn and brown on the other side; when done, dust with sugar, roll quickly. Serve hot with jelly for sauce.

French Pancakes. Beat the yolks of 4 eggs very light; add to 4 cups sifted flour with enough milk and water to make a thin batter; beat perfectly smooth; add 2 tablespoonfuls olive oil, 1 tablespoonful French brandy and ½ teaspoonful salt; let stand 2 or 3 hours. When ready to use add 1 heaping teaspoonful Rumford Yeast Powder, mix well. Place 1 tablespoonful butter or oil in a frying-pan, put over the fire and when smoking-hot pour in enough batter to cover the bottom of the pan; brown on both sides, dust with powdered sugar. Serve at once on hot dish.

Puff Balls. Beat 3 eggs very light; add 2 cups milk and ¼ teaspoonful salt; pour this very gradually into 2 cups of flour sifted with 1 heaping teaspoonful Rumford Yeast Powder; beat constantly. You should have a perfectly smooth batter. Heat the gem pans very hot, brush well with butter or oil, fill half full; bake in a quick oven 30 minutes. These are nice for breakfast, or served with lemon sauce.

Sally Lunn. Beat yolks of 2 eggs, 2 tablespoonfuls sugar and ½ cup butter together until light; add 1 cup milk and enough flour to make a stiff cake batter; beat smooth. Add whites of eggs beaten to a stiff froth and 1 heaping teaspoonful Rumford Yeast Powder; pour into greased cake pan (with cylinder,) and bake ¾ hour in a moderate oven. Serve hot.

FRITTERS.

Plain Fritters. Add ½ teaspoonful salt to 1½ cups flour and sift into a bowl; beat the yolks of 2 eggs slightly, add gradually ½ cup cold water and beat briskly until light and foamy; add ½ cup milk and mix well. Make a hole in the centre of the flour, add the liquid very slowly, stirring constantly; beat until perfectly smooth, then mix in carefully 1 heaping teaspoonful Rumford Yeast Powder and the whites of the eggs beaten to a froth. Fry in smoking-hot fat a few minutes, until a rich brown; drain and dust with sugar.

Fruit Fritters. Use Plain Fritter Batter with the addition of a little sugar, using any kind of ripe fruit, sliced or chopped fine and mixed or dipped in the batter.

Egg Fritters. Put 2 cups water and ½ cup good, fresh butter in a saucepan over the fire; when it boils add 2 teaspoonfuls sugar and throw in 2 cups well-sifted flour; stir rapidly until it forms a stiff ball of paste and leaves the side of the saucepan; cook a few minutes, but do not allow it to burn; then set away to cool. When quite cold add 6 eggs, breaking in 1 at a time and beating it in until thoroughly mixed; then beat the dough vigorously until very light, (about 5 minutes), add 1 teaspoonful Rumford Yeast Powder; mix well; drop small spoonfuls into deep, hot fat and fry 3 minutes, take out and drain on soft paper, dust with sugar and cinnamon; serve hot. Canned peaches are delicious in these; place ½ a peach in each spoonful of batter and use the juice as sauce.

Colonial Fritters. Scald 1 quart milk; pour it over 2 cups fine bread crumbs, add 1 tablespoonful butter, cover and soak 1 hour; then beat to a paste, add yolks of 3 eggs well-beaten, 2 cups flour, ½ teaspoonful salt, 2 tablespoonfuls sugar, ¼ teaspoonful each of grated nutmeg and cinnamon, beat well; add 1 rounded teaspoonful Rumford Yeast Powder, 1 cup currants, (floured), and the whites of the eggs beaten stiff. Fry 3 minutes in deep hot fat; drain and roll in powdered sugar and cinnamon. Serve hot with wine sauce.

Corn Oyster Fritters. One dozen ears sweet corn; score through the centre of each row of kernels and press out the pulp with a fork; add 3 eggs well-beaten, 1 cup milk, 1 teaspoonful salt, 2 dashes pepper, about 1½ cups flour and 1 rounded teaspoonful Rumford Yeast Powder. Fry in deep hot fat; drain and serve very hot.

Potato Fritters. To 2 cups cold mashed potato add 1 cup milk, 2 well-beaten eggs, 1 teaspoonful salt, 2 cups flour and 2 heaping teaspoonfuls Rumford Yeast Powder. Put a small quantity of fat in a frying-pan and when smoking-hot dip the batter out by tablespoonfuls; brown well on one side, then turn and brown on the other. Serve while hot.

Oyster Fritters. Wipe dry as many oysters as you wish fritters. Make a batter as follows: Beat well 1 egg; add to it 1 cup milk, ½ teaspoonful salt, 1 pint flour and 1 heaping teaspoonful Rumford Yeast Powder. Put a small quantity of fat in a frying-pan; dip oysters one by one in the batter, and when the fat is smoking-hot drop oysters in and fry brown, first on one side and then on the other. Serve hot.

Clam Fritters. Clam Fritters may be made in the same way as Oyster Fritters, or they may be chopped fine, rejecting all hard parts, mixed with the batter and dropped by spoonfuls into smoking-hot fat.

Bell Fritters. Beat well the yolks of 4 eggs; add to them 1 cup cold water, 2 tablespoonfuls melted butter, 1 teaspoonful salt. Pour this into 1 pint flour, then add the well-beaten whites of the eggs, and drop by spoonfuls into smoking-hot fat. Brown first on one side and then on the other. While hot dust with powdered sugar and serve.

Banana Fritters. Separate 2 eggs; to the yolks add 2 tablespoonfuls melted butter, ¼ teaspoonful salt, ⅔ cup water, 1 pint flour. Stir in carefully the whites of eggs beaten to a stiff, dry froth, and 1 heaping teaspoonful Rumford Yeast Powder. Cut the bananas in quarters, dip in the batter and fry in smoking-hot fat.

Apricot Fritters. Prepare the batter as in Banana Fritters. Cut the apricots into halves, dip in batter and fry as in Banana Fritters. Dust with powdered sugar and serve.

DOUGHNUTS and CRULLERS.

Doughnuts. To 3 eggs well-beaten add ¼ cup milk. Into 2 cups flour rub 1 tablespoonful butter; add ½ teaspoonful salt and 1 heaping teaspoonful Rumford Yeast Powder. Mix all well together, knead lightly on board, roll out about ½ inch thick, cut with round cutter and fry in smoking-hot fat. Brown well, and while hot dust with powdered sugar.

Dunkale Doughnuts. Beat 1 cup sugar and 1 egg together until very light; add 1 cup milk, ½ teaspoonful salt, 3 tablespoonfuls melted butter, 1 heaping teaspoonful Rumford Yeast Powder and sufficient flour to make a *very* soft dough. Turn out with a spoon a small quantity at a time on a well-floured board, dredge with flour roll out ¼ inch thick, cut into small rings and fry in sufficient smoking-hot fat to cover them. Drain and dredge with sugar.

New York Crullers. Cream 2 tablespoonfuls butter and 1 cup sugar. Add to it 3 eggs well-beaten, ⅔ cup water and grated nutmeg to taste. Sift into 1 quart flour 2 heaping teaspoonfuls Rumford Yeast Powder. Mix all well together; roll out on board about one-quarter of an inch thick. Cut out with a large round cutter, then with a smaller one, making circles. Twist them into figure eights, press in middle to keep from falling apart, drop in smoking-hot fat and brown first on one side and then on the other. Drain on brown paper and dust while hot with powdered sugar.

MEAT DISHES.

Cottage Pie. Put 1 pound cold boiled mutton, 4 good-sized cold boiled potatoes cut into small pieces, into a deep baking dish; add 1 cup stock or broth from the mutton, salt, pepper and a sprinkling of mint. Cut 1 ounce butter over the top and cover with paste made as follows; 1 cup mashed potato, 1 tablespoonful butter, ½ teaspoonful salt, a little pepper, ¼ cup cream, and white of 1 egg, beat all together until very light, add 1 teaspoonful Rumford Yeast Powder to 1 cup flour and work all together into a soft dough, handling as little as possible. Pat into a round sheet about one-half inch thick, make an opening in the middle, place over the pie and brush with the yolk of egg. Bake in a moderately hot oven 1 hour.

Meat Tasties. Make with Potato Paste, or well-shortened Biscuit dough. Roll thin, cut out size of a small saucer; partly fill with a savory meat hash; brush edges of crust with white of egg, fold them over, slightly pinch edges together and brush the tops with yolk of egg; bake in a quick oven 30 minutes. Serve with brown sauce.

Egg Dumplings. Sift together 1 pound flour, 1 heaping teaspoonful Rumford Yeast Powder and ½ teaspoonful salt; add to this 2 eggs beaten light and sufficient cold water to make a soft dough; drop into boiling, salted water, cover closely and steam 12 or 15 minutes. Serve as a garnish for a meat stew. Drop Dumplings must steam 10 minutes before the cover is removed or they will fall and be heavy.

Savory Stew with Dumplings. Cut into pieces about 1 inch square, 2 pounds of the shoulder of beef. Roll each piece well in flour; place in a pan with 2 tablespoonfuls drippings or butter, and fry until a nice brown. Remove the meat, put it in a saucepan; then fry 2 small onions, sliced, 1 carrot and 1 turnip cut into dice, and when well browned put into the saucepan with the meat. Mix 2 tablespoonfuls flour with the fat remaining in the frying-pan; add to it 1 quart water, 2 teaspoonfuls salt, and pepper to taste. Pour this over the meat in the saucepan; add to it 1 bayleaf, 3 cloves, 1 sprig parsley, 1 stalk celery and ½ teaspoonful sweet marjoram. Cover and let simmer until meat is tender. About 15 minutes before serving, sift together 1 pint flour, 1 teaspoonful salt and 1 heaping teaspoonful Rumford Yeast Powder. Mix with enough milk or water to make a soft dough, and drop by spoonfuls into the stew. Cover tightly and cook for about 10 minutes. Serve immediately.

Lenten or Sea Pie. Line the rim of a pie dish with plain pie crust. Cut into small pieces about 2 pounds of halibut, haddock, salmon, or any fish from which the bones may be easily removed. Put the fish in the pie dish and sprinkle with 1 teaspoonful salt, a little cayenne, ½ teaspoonful curry powder and 1 tablespoonful chopped parsley. Put 1 tablespoonful butter in a frying-pan and when well browned add 1 tablespoonful flour; mix well and add ½ pint milk and ½ teaspoonful salt. Stir until it thickens and then pour over the fish. Now cover loosely with the pie crust, making one or two small openings in centre to allow steam to escape; press down well around lower part of rim, place in very hot oven and bake until a nice brown.

PASTRY and PIES.

In making pastry, success depends greatly on having all materials very cold, and the heat of your oven at the proper temperature, about as hot as for rolls, with a strong underheat. If butter is used entirely, the pastry will be much improved by washing it well in cold water before mixing with the flour.

Plain Cheap Pie Crust. Sift together 1 pint pastry flour, ½ teaspoonful salt, ½ teaspoonful Rumford Yeast Powder. Then cut into the flour 2 heaping tablespoonfuls butter and lard mixed, and mix with enough ice-cold water (about one-half cup), to moisten, not wet, the flour and shortening. Roll out on board, turn in the sides and ends, fold, place on the board with folds at sides, and roll once or twice more, or until smooth.

Suet Paste for Meat Pies. Put 1 pound flour in a mixing bowl and add to it 1 teaspoonful salt. Remove the skin from ½ pound beef suet and chop it fine, mixing a little of the flour with it to keep it from lumping. When well chopped, mix with the flour and add by degrees enough ice water to form a stiff paste; knead lightly on board and let stand about 10 minutes, when it is ready to use.

Raised or Lard Paste. Put 1 cup lard in a small saucepan, place over the hot part of stove and as soon as it stops bub-

bling, remove, strain and set away to cool. With 1 quart of
flour sift well 1 teaspoonful salt and 2 teaspoonfuls Rumford
Yeast Powder, and when the lard is cold and hard cut it up in
the flour into pieces about one-half inch square. Now add carefully and by degrees enough ice-water to moisten—not wet, the
flour. Turn out on the board and pat down lightly with the
rolling-pin. Turn in the sides and ends and fold in two; turn
on the board so that the folds will be at the side. Roll out in
the same way once or twice, or until smooth.

Plain Puff Paste. Place in a bowl 8 ounces flour and 6 of
butter; chop into pieces about one inch square. Make a well
in centre and in it place the yolk of 1 egg, ¼ saltspoonful salt,
1 teaspoonful lemon juice and 1 tablespoonful ice water. Now
with the fingers mix lightly and form into a stiff paste, using
more flour if necessary. Roll out on board into an oblong
sheet about one-half inch thick, fold one-third over, then the
other third over that, turn on board so that folds will be at
side, roll again and it is ready for use, but will be improved by
standing in a cold place a short time before using. *This is said
to be the recipe used by the South Kensington School of Cookery, and followed exactly will be quite satisfactory.*

Rich Puff Paste. Wash 1 pound good sweet butter in ice
water for about 5 minutes. Press the water out of it by squeez-
ing in a cloth, then place in the ice-box until thoroughly cold
and *hard.* Put 1 pound flour in a bowl, make a well in the centre and place in it 1 ounce of the butter, the white of 1 egg
beaten slightly, and 1 teaspoonful salt. Mix lightly with the
fingers into a paste, working the flour in (except a little saved
for dredging), by degrees, with about 1 cup ice water. When
well mixed, knead until smooth and firm. Now roll this out
into an oblong sheet about one-half inch thick; take the rest of
the butter from the ice-box (if thoroughly cold) wipe it dry,
break into pieces and place on one half the sheet, dredge with
flour, fold other half over the butter, press down round the edge
so the butter cannot escape. Now pat down lightly with the
rolling-pin, turn in sides and ends with knife, fold in two, turn
on board so that folds are at side, roll out again, fold in ends
to middle of sheet (not sides this time), then fold in two, turn
on board with folds at side, wrap in cheese-cloth and place in
ice-box ½ hour. Then roll out in the same way 6 times, placing in ice-box for ⅓ hour between each two rollings. This
paste may be kept for a week. It should not be used the same
day it is made, as it is then hard to manage and apt to shrink.
It should be baked in a very hot oven.

Pâte-à-Chou. Put 1 cup water in a saucepan; place over
the fire; as soon as it boils add 2 ounces good, sweet butter;
stir until well mixed, then throw in 8 rounded tablespoonfuls (1

cup), well-sifted flour; stir quickly over the fire, until it forms a smooth ball of paste, leaving the sides of the saucepan; stir well and cook 5 minutes; set aside to cool. When cold break into it 4 eggs, one at a time, thoroughly beating each one in before adding the next; then beat briskly for 5 minutes and stand aside until ready to use. Add, just before baking, 1 heaping teaspoonful Rumford Yeast Powder.

Cherry Pie. Line a deep pie dish with Plain Cheap Pie Crust rolled thin; fill with freshly picked, stoned, tart cherries, heaping them in the centre; sprinkle over them 1 cup sugar; brush the rim *near* the edge with a little water; cover with a thin upper crust, making an opening in the centre for steam to escape; bake in a steady, quick oven 25 minutes.

Peach Pie. Line a deep pie dish with paste. Pare and stone nice ripe peaches; arrange in the dish stone side down, sprinkle well with sugar; add 2 tablespoonfuls water; arrange narrow strips of paste across the top, fastening lightly at each end; brush the rim with water, finish with a strip of paste around the margin; glaze with egg yolk and bake in a quick oven 25 minutes.

Scotch Apple Tart. Pare, halve and remove cores from 6 fine, tart apples; arrange in a pie dish lined with Raised or Lard Paste; sprinkle the apples with cinnamon and sugar; chop 1 large tablespoonful butter into small pieces; spread over the apples; add 2 tablespoonfuls water. Bake in a quick oven 25 or 30 minutes. When done spread over the top a thick layer of Scotch marmalade. Serve with cream.

Apple Pie. Pare and grate, fine tart apples; add 1 tablespoonful butter, melted, for each pie; sweeten to taste, flavor with nutmeg and grated rind and juice of lemon; line pie plates with crust; fill with the mixture, cover with a thin top crust or cross bars of paste; bake in a moderately quick oven 30 minutes.

Strawberry Meringue Pie. Line a pie plate with Raised or Lard Paste; put a second strip around the rim. Bake in a very hot oven until light brown. Remove from oven and while hot fill with strawberries. Beat whites of 2 eggs and 3 tablespoonfuls sugar together until stiff. Place in little mounds over the strawberries, sprinkle with granulated sugar, and place in oven about 1 minute or until light brown.

Neapolitan Short Cake. Take some Rich Puff Paste and roll out into three very thin sheets about eight inches wide and ten long. Place these on top of each other and bake in very hot oven until light brown. Remove from oven, separate into three layers; on lower layer place apricots cut in halves, slightly mashed and thickly sprinkled with sugar. Place another layer of short cake over this and cover with strawberries slightly mashed and well sugared. Place third layer of short cake on this and spread with grated pineapple thickly sprinkled with sugar. On top of all spread oranges cut into dice, or sliced bananas and whipped-cream.

Lemon Custard Pie. Beat the yolks of 3 eggs, add gradually 1 cup sugar, beat well, then add 1 heaping tablespoonful corn-starch, the grated yellow rind and juice of 1 lemon and 1 cup milk. Line a pie plate with pie crust, placing an extra strip around the rim. Pour in the lemon custard mixture and bake in hot oven. Beat the whites of eggs to a froth, add 3 tablespoonfuls powdered sugar, beat until stiff. Place in little mounds over the pie, sprinkle with granulated sugar and put back in oven to brown, 1 minute being sufficient if the oven is hot.

Apple Custard. Prepare a sauce with 6 large, tart apples; add while hot 2 ounces butter. When cold, add 1 cup milk, a little salt, nutmeg and the grated peel and juice of 1 lemon, sugar to taste and 3 eggs beaten light; mix well together; turn into deep pie-plates lined with Plain Puff Paste. Bake in a quick oven until the paste is a nice brown and the custard is set.

Orange Custard Pie. Beat yolks of 3 eggs; add gradually 1 cup sugar. Then add the grated yellow rind of 1 and juice of ½ an orange, 1 heaping tablespoonful corn-starch and 1 cup milk. Line a pie plate with pie crust; place an extra strip around the rim, pour in the orange custard mixture and bake in hot oven. Beat the whites of eggs to froth, add 3 tablespoonfuls powdered sugar, beat until stiff; place over the pie in little mounds, sprinkle with granulated sugar, and put in oven for about a minute to brown.

Banana Pie. Line a pie plate with pie crust. Cut 3 or 4 bananas into slices, place in the pie, sprinkle with sugar and small pieces of orange or pineapple. Cover with an upper crust and bake until a nice brown.

Tomato Pie. Scald enough green tomatoes to make 1 pound when pared; let them stand a few minutes; then remove the skins, slice rather thick, cover with ¾ cup brown sugar, 1 tablespoonful molasses and a piece of ginger root. Cook until tender, then place in a deep dish lined with Plain Puff Paste; put slices of lemon on top, cover with a thin top crust and bake in a quick oven 25 minutes.

Patty Shells. Roll out 1 pound Rich Puff Paste one-third of an inch thick; for each patty cut out 3 rounds with a large pastry cutter; place rounds on top of one another, brushing the two lower ones *near* the edges with white of egg to hold all together; be careful not to press edges together or they will not rise. Now, with a *very* small cutter dipped in flour, cut the centres from the two upper rounds, but do not remove them until after the patties are baked. Glaze with yolk of egg and bake in a quick oven until perfectly light, about 15 minutes. These are used for oysters, sweet-bread or any sweet patties.

Christmas Mince Pie.

Chop very fine 1 pound lean, boiled beef, 2½ pounds tart apples, ½ pound beef suet, ½ pound citron and candied orange peel; mix all together and add ½ pound sultanas, 1 pound layer raisins, seeded, 1 pound washed currants, 1½ pounds light brown sugar, a little salt, 1 grated nutmeg, juice and grated rind of 2 lemons, 1 teaspoonful each of mace, cloves, cinnamon, allspice and ginger, 1 pint boiled cider or grape juice, and 1 pint good brandy; mix thoroughly; pack in stone or glass jars and set away in a cold place. This will keep for months and should be made some time before needed for pies. Bake with either Plain Puff Paste or Rich Puff Paste, in rather shallow dishes, with a top crust.

Pâte-à-la-Crême.

Roll out a piece of Rich Puff Paste one-quarter inch thick; trim with a sharp knife to the size of a large pie plate; lay it on a baking tin. Make an even, flat border all around the margin with Pâte-à-chou paste pressed through a pastry tube or arranged with a spoon; glaze with beaten egg, dust with powdered sugar and bake in a very quick oven 25 or 30 minutes. Place on another baking sheet 18 or 20 little round cakes of the chou paste, glaze, sprinkle with chopped almonds and powdered sugar; bake in a quick oven 15 minutes. When the pâte shell is baked and cold, fill with vanilla cream, and garnish the border with the little balls, candied cherries, green grapes, etc.

Vanilla Cream.

Soak ¼ box gelatine in enough cold water to cover it. Whip 1 pint good cream and lay it on a sieve to drain; then turn into a basin and place on cracked ice. Fold into the cream very carefully 4 tablespoonfuls powdered sugar, ½ teaspoonful vanilla, 4 tablespoonfuls sherry and the gelatine dissolved in a very little warm water, and strained. Stir until it *begins* to thicken, when it is done.

SMALL CAKES.

Frost Cookies.

Cream ¼ cup butter; add to it gradually 1 cup sugar. Beat well for about 5 minutes, then add ½ cup milk, 1 heaping teaspoonful Rumford Yeast Powder and enough flour to make a smooth dough. Roll out on board, cut out with round biscuit or cake cutter, sprinkle thickly with coarse granulated sugar and bake in a very moderate oven; do not brown.

Vanilla Drops. Cream ½ cup butter and 2 cups sugar; add 2 eggs well-beaten, ¾ cup water, 2 heaping teaspoonfuls Rumford Yeast Powder and enough flour to make a very stiff batter. Flavor with vanilla sugar or essence of vanilla to taste; drop on a well-greased baking pan and bake in a moderately quick oven until a light brown.

Cocoanut Cookies. Cream ½ cup butter with 1 cup sugar; add to it 2 eggs, well-beaten, ¼ cup milk, 1 cup cocoanut, 1 heaping teaspoonful Rumford Yeast Powder. Stir in enough flour to make stiff enough to roll. Roll out on a board, cut with cake-cutter and bake in a quick oven.

Ginger Crisps. Mix together ½ cup butter, ½ cup sugar, 1 cup molasses, 2 heaping teaspoonfuls Rumford Yeast Powder, 2 level teaspoonfuls ginger, and flour to make stiff enough to roll. Roll out very thin; cut with round cutter and bake in hot oven, until well browned.

Five O'clock Teas. Beat ½ cup butter, 1½ cups powdered sugar and the yolks of 4 eggs together until very light; then add 1 cup water and 1½ cups sifted flour; beat until perfectly smooth. Beat egg whites to a stiff froth, fold in carefully; then add another 1½ cups flour in which have been sifted 2 teaspoonfuls Rumford Yeast Powder; mix well. Drop by half teaspoonfuls into a well-buttered baking tin; the batter must not be thin enough to run; bake in a moderate oven 10 minutes. When done trim a uniform size with a small biscuit cutter or tin box lid; make into little jelly cakes by spreading them with different kinds of jelly and marmalade; ice with different-colored icing flavored to correspond with the filling.

CAKE.

Success in cake baking depends on care and accuracy in measuring ingredients, fresh eggs, good butter and the best pastry flour—straight winter wheat flour. If you use the ordinary flour your batter may be too thick and cause the cake to crack open; in this case use a smaller quantity than called for. Too hot an oven will make the cake crack open.

One Egg Cake. One cup sugar and 2 tablespoonfuls butter, beaten to a cream. Beat 1 egg very light; add to it 1 cup cold water and beat until it foams. Mix with the sugar and butter; add a little salt, and 1 heaping teaspoonful Rumford Yeast Powder sifted through 2½ cups flour; add flavoring; mix thoroughly, and bake in a moderately quick oven 45 minutes.

Rumford Jelly Cake. Beat 1 cup butter, 2 cups sugar and yolks of 4 eggs together until light; then add 1 cup milk and 2 cups sifted flour; beat hard until smooth, then add ¼ tea-spoonful mace, 2 tablespoonfuls brandy, the well-beaten whites, 2 heaping teaspoonfuls Rumford Yeast Powder thoroughly sifted through 2 more cups flour; mix well; do not beat; turn into layer cake pans and bake in a moderately quick oven 15 minutes. When done, remove from pans, cool, and spread layers with jelly or crushed fruit. Dust the top layer with powdered sugar.

Café Noir Cake. Cream 2 cups brown sugar with 1 cup butter; add the well-beaten yolks of 5 eggs, then 1-4 teaspoon-ful nutmeg, 1 teaspoonful cinnamon, ¼ teaspoonful cloves, 1 cup of very strong, freshly made coffee, 4 cups flour; stir in 1 cup stoned raisins, 1 cup currants, ¼ pound citron well-floured, and 2 heaping teaspoonfuls Rumford Yeast Powder sifted and mixed in carefully and thoroughly. Bake in a moderate oven 1 hour. This will make two loaf cakes.

Marble Cake. *For the white portion.* Cream 1 cup butter with 3 of white sugar, then add 1 cup milk, 5 cups flour, 1 heap-ing teaspoonful Rumford Yeast Powder. Stir in carefully the whites of 8 eggs beaten to a stiff froth, and flavor with lemon.

For the dark portion. Cream 1 cup butter, and add to it 3 cups brown sugar, 1 cup molasses, 1 cup milk, 4 cups flour, 2 heaping teaspoonfuls Rumford Yeast Powder. Then stir in yolks of 8 eggs and 1 whole one. Flavor with cinnamon, nut-meg and clove.

Put into well-greased cake pans, alternate layers of dark and light parts, having bottom and top layers dark. Bake in moderate oven.

Plain Cake. Beat together until very light, 1 cup sugar and yolks of 2 eggs; add 6 tablespoonfuls water, then 1 cup flour and 1 teaspoonful Rumford Yeast Powder sifted together. Fold in carefully the well-beaten whites. Bake in a moderately quick oven 25 or 30 minutes.

Soft Gingerbread. Cream ⅔ cup lard; add the beaten yolks of 2 eggs; beat until light; add ⅔ cup milk stirred into 2 cups New Orleans molasses, 1 level teaspoonful cinnamon, ½ teaspoonful ginger, 1 teaspoonful salt, 1 heaping tea-spoonful Rumford Yeast Powder sifted with 3 cups flour, and the whites of eggs beaten stiff. Bake in a long, shallow biscuit pan in a moderate oven 40 minutes.

White Fruit Cake. Beat together until white and creamy, ½ cup butter and 1 cup sugar. Then add 2 whole eggs, one at a time, beating each one in very thoroughly. Add ½ cup milk or water. Sift 2 cups pastry flour, add half to the batter;

then add 1 cup sliced citron, ½ cup currants, ½ teaspoonful
vanilla, and remainder of the flour sifted with 2 teaspoonfuls
Rumford Yeast Powder. Bake in a moderate oven 1 hour.

Ice Cream Cake. Beat to a white cream 1 cup butter and
3 cups sugar; add 1 cup water and mix well; then add ½ teaspoonful rose-water. Sift 2 cups flour and 1 heaping teaspoonful Rumford Yeast Powder together twice and add to batter;
then stir in very carefully the well-beaten whites of 6 eggs. Bake
in layers in a quick oven 15 minutes. Spread layers with Plain
Boiled Icing; ice top and sides with same, and sprinkle with
finely-chopped almonds.

Gold Cake. Cream ½ cup butter and 1½ cups light brown
sugar; add 1 cup water, the yolks of 4 eggs, about 3 cups flour,
and 2 heaping teaspoonfuls Rumford Yeast Powder. Flavor
with vanilla.

Silver Cake. Cream ½ cup butter with 1½ cups white sugar;
add ½ cup milk, 2½ cups flour, 1 heaping teaspoonful Rumford
Yeast Powder. Stir in carefully the whites of 6 eggs beaten to
a stiff froth. Flavor with almond.

Snow Bound Cake. Cream ½ cup butter; add to it 2 cups
sugar, ½ cup milk, about 2 cups flour, 1 heaping teaspoonful
Rumford Yeast Powder. Stir in the well-beaten whites of 3
eggs. Bake in a moderate oven about ¾ of an hour. Beat up
the whites of 2 eggs and 3 tablespoonfuls powdered sugar until
stiff; spread over the cake, covering top and sides completely;
then sprinkle thickly with grated cocoanut. Stand away to
dry.

Fruit Lunch. Cream ½ cup butter; add to it 2 cups sugar,
1 of milk, 3 eggs, well-beaten, grated peel of ½ a lemon, 3 cups
flour and 2 heaping teaspoonfuls Rumford Yeast Powder. Now
stir in ⅔ cup candied pineapple and citron, and bake in a
moderate oven ¾ of an hour.

Nugat Cake. Cream 1 cup butter with 1½ cups sugar;
add 1 cup water or milk; flavor with orange-flower water or
grated peel of orange; add 3 cups flour sifted with 1 heaping
teaspoonful Rumford Yeast Powder. Mix carefully, then fold in
the well-beaten whites of 5 eggs. Bake in 3 layers in a moderately quick oven 20 minutes. When done make a boiled icing;
stir into it chopped nuts of different kinds and spread between
the layers. Dust the top well with powdered sugar.

Colonial Sponge Cake. Separate 6 eggs; beat the yolks
and 1½ cups sugar until very, very light; then add 8 tablespoonfuls of hot water and beat again; add juice and grated

rind of 1 lemon. Now stir in very carefully 1½ cups sifted flour, alternating it with the whites of eggs beaten to a stiff froth; add 1 heaping teaspoonful Rumford Yeast Powder sifted with the last addition of flour. Do not *beat* sponge cake batter after adding the flour and whites of the eggs, or the cake will be heavy. Bake in a shallow, square pan in a quick, steady oven for 35 minutes.

Chocolate Nut Cake. *Light Part.*

Beat together until very light 1 cup of sugar and ¼ cup butter; add 6 tablespoonfuls milk, ½ teaspoonful vanilla, 1 heaping teaspoonful Rumford Yeast Powder sifted with 1½ cups flour, and the well-beaten whites of 4 eggs. Bake in two layers.

Dark Part. One-half cup sugar, 3 ounces butter and yolks of 4 eggs beaten together; add 1 ounce grated chocolate, ¼ cup milk, 1 rounded teaspoonful Rumford Yeast Powder and 1 cup flour. Mix well and bake in one layer.

Make filling as follows: 4 ounces chocolate melted; add ½ cup cream, 2 tablespoonfuls butter and 1 cup sugar; boil until it forms a very soft ball when dropped in ice water; then add 1 cup finely chopped nuts. Spread this very thick between the layers. Ice with plain chocolate icing and decorate with unbroken halves of English Walnuts.

Orange Cake.

Cream 1 cup butter; add to it gradually 2 cups sugar, 4 eggs, 1 cup water, 3 cups flour and 2 heaping teaspoonfuls Rumford Yeast Powder. Bake in layers and spread each layer with orange-filling. Put together and spread on top with orange-icing. Around the edge of the cake lay slices of orange cut into halves, from which the skin has not been removed, and place so as to form scallops.

Orange Filling. Mix 1 cup sugar, grated rind and juice of 1 orange, 2 tablespoonfuls flour and 1 egg. Cook until smooth and creamy.

Christmas Fruit Cake.

Cream 1 cup butter, 2 of brown sugar; add 1 cup molasses, 1 cup sweet milk, 3 eggs, 5 cups flour, 2 heaping teaspoonfuls Rumford Yeast Powder. Then add 1 tablespoonful each cinnamon and nutmeg. Flour well 1 pound raisins, 1 pound dried currants and ¼ pound dried citron. Stir this into the cake. Put the batter into two well-greased cake pans and bake in a moderate oven 2 hours.

Berry Tea Cake.

Beat 3 eggs until light. Add 1 cup sugar; 1 cup milk, 2 tablespoonfuls melted butter, 2 heaping teaspoonfuls Rumford Yeast Powder, and enough flour to make a stiff batter. Stir in 1 cup raspberries or any which may be in season. Pour into well-greased cake pan and bake in a very hot oven ¾ of an hour.

New York Fruit Cake. Beat 1 pound butter to a cream; add 1 pound light brown sugar and beat until very light; add the well-beaten yolks of 8 eggs; then 1 pound of flour mixed with ½ teaspoonful mace, 1 teaspoonful cinnamon, ½ teaspoonful cloves and 1 nutmeg; give the batter a vigorous beating; seed 1 pound raisins, slice ½ pound citron, clean 1 pound sultanas and 1 pound currants; add to the batter with juice and grated rind of 1 orange and 1 lemon; mix thoroughly; sift in carefully 3 large dessert-spoonfuls Rumford Yeast Powder; then stir in the beaten whites. Bake in 2 round cake pans lined with greased paper. They will require 4 hours in a very moderate oven.

Fruit Cake. Cream ¼ cup butter, add gradually ¾ cup brown sugar, ½ cup molasses, 3 egg yolks and 1 egg well beaten, 1 cup raisins, stoned and cut into pieces, 1 tablespoonful brandy and ¼ cup milk. Mix and sift 2¼ cups flour, 2 teaspoonfuls Rumford Yeast Powder, ½ teaspoonful salt, ½ teaspoonful cinnamon and ¼ nutmeg, grated, and add to the first mixture. Bake in a moderate oven 1 hour.

Cheap Sponge Cake. Beat the yolks of 2 eggs until thick, add gradually 1 cup sugar and ½ teaspoonful extract lemon, and beat. Add ⅔ cup hot water, whites of the eggs beaten to a stiff froth, and 1 cup flour mixed with 1 teaspoonful Rumford Yeast Powder and ¼ teaspoonful salt, sifted. Bake in buttered cake pan 45 minutes.

Cornstarch Cake. Cream ¼ cup butter, add gradually 1 cup sugar, ¼ teaspoonful almond extract, the whites of 2 eggs beaten to a stiff froth, and ¼ cup cornstarch mixed with ¼ cup milk. Sift together ¾ cup flour and 1 teaspoonful Rumford Yeast Powder and add. Bake in a narrow, deep cake pan 35 minutes.

French Cake. Cream ½ cup butter, add gradually 1 cup sugar, ¾ teaspoonful vanilla, ¼ teaspoonful lemon, and ½ cup raisins, stoned and chopped. Beat the whites of 3 eggs to a stiff froth and add. Mix and sift 2 cups flour and 2 teaspoonfuls Rumford Yeast Powder; add to the first mixture alternately with ⅓ cup milk. Bake in a moderate oven 40 minutes. Cover with boiling frosting.

Light Fruit Cake. Cream ¼ cup butter, add gradually 1 cup sugar, ½ cup raisins, stoned and chopped fine, 2 ounces citron cut fine, and ⅓ cup walnuts cut in pieces. Beat the whites of 4 eggs to a stiff froth and add. Mix and sift 2 cups flour and 2 teaspoonfuls Rumford Yeast Powder; add to the first mixture alternately with ⅓ cup milk. Bake in a moderate oven 40 minutes.

Spanish Cake. To 2 tablespoonfuls melted butter add gradually 1 cup sugar. Add ½ teaspoonful cinnamon and 3 egg yolks, beaten until light-colored. Mix and sift 2 scant cups flour and 1½ teaspoonfuls Rumford Yeast Powder; add alternately with ½ cup milk to the first mixture. Bake in layers. Spread caramel frosting between and on top.

Cream Cake. Break 2 eggs into a bowl, add ⅔ cup cream and 1 cup sugar, and beat vigorously. Mix and sift 1¾ cups flour, ½ teaspoonful salt, 1½ teaspoonfuls Rumford Yeast Powder, ½ teaspoonful cinnamon, ¼ teaspoonful mace, ¼ teaspoonful ginger, and add to the first mixture.

Swiss Cake. Cream ½ cup butter, add gradually 2 cups sugar; add 4 eggs well beaten. Mix and sift 3½ cups flour and 2 teaspoonfuls Rumford Yeast Powder, ½ teaspoonful soda, ½ teaspoonful salt, 1½ teaspoonfuls cinnamon and ¾ teaspoonful ginger; add alternately with 1 cup sour milk to the first mixture.

Bride's Cake. Cream ½ cup butter, add gradually 1½ cups sugar; add ½ teaspoonful almond extract. Mix and sift 2¼ cups flour and 2 teaspoonfuls Rumford Yeast Powder; add alternately with ½ cup milk to the first mixture, also 6 egg whites. Bake in a deep cake pan 55 minutes.

Bridal Cake. Cream ½ cup butter, add gradually 1 cup sugar and ⅓ cup milk. Mix and sift 1¾ cups flour and 2 teaspoonfuls Rumford Yeast Powder, and add. Beat 1 egg yolk until thick; beat 3 egg whites until stiff. Add the eggs to the mixture. Bake thoroughly.

Chocolate Cake. Cream 2 tablespoonfuls butter, add gradually 1 cup sugar; add 1 well beaten egg. Mix and sift 1¼ cups flour and 1 teaspoonful Rumford Yeast Powder; add alternately with ½ cup milk to the first mixture. Add ½ teaspoonful vanilla and 1 square chocolate, melted, just before putting into the pan.

Chocolate Nugat Cake. Cream 2 tablespoonfuls butter, add gradually 1½ cups sugar; add 1 well beaten egg. Mix and sift 2¼ cups flour and 2½ teaspoonfuls Rumford Yeast Powder; add alternately with 1 cup milk to the first mixture. Add 3 squares chocolate, melted, and 1 cup shredded almonds just before putting into the pan. Bake in layers, and put White Mountain Cream between layers and on top.

Raisin Cake. Cream 1 cup butter, add gradually 2 cups sugar and 1 cup raisins, stoned and cut into pieces; add 1 cup cold water and a scant 2¼ cups flour. Beat 4 egg whites until stiff; beat the egg yolks until thick. Beat the whites and yolks together and add to the fruit mixture. Add scant 2¼ cups flour mixed and sifted with 4 teaspoonfuls Rumford Yeast Powder.

Currant Cake. Cream ½ cup butter, add gradually 1 cup sugar; add ¾ cup currants. Add 2 eggs well beaten and ¼ cup milk. Mix and sift 1¾ cups flour and 2 teaspoonfuls Rumford Yeast Powder and add. Beat vigorously. Bake in a sheet 45 minutes. Remove from the pan and sprinkle with powdered sugar.

Date Cake. Mix ½ cup butter, 1½ cups brown sugar, ½ cup milk. 2 eggs, 1¾ cups flour, 2 teaspoonfuls Rumford Yeast Powder. ½ teaspoonful cinnamon, ½ teaspoonful nutmeg. ½ pound dates, stoned and cut into pieces. Beat for 2 minutes. The butter must be soft to combine readily. Known as "Quick Cake."

Walnut Cake. Cream ½ cup butter, add gradually 1 cup sugar; add ¾ cup walnut meat broken into pieces. Add 2 egg whites and 3 egg yolks well beaten, and ½ cup milk. Mix and sift 1½ cups flour and 1½ teaspoonfuls Rumford Yeast Powder, and add. Beat vigorously. Bake as Currant Cake. Cover with White Mountain Cream.

Ribbon Cake. Cream ½ cup butter, add gradually 2 cups sugar and the well beaten yolks of 4 eggs. Add 1 cup milk, 3½ cups flour mixed and sifted with 3 teaspoonfuls Rumford Yeast Powder. Add the egg whites beaten to a stiff froth. Bake one-half of the mixture in a layer cake pan. To the remainder add ½ pound figs, chopped fine, ½ cup raisins, stoned and cut into pieces. 1 tablespoonful molasses, and spices to taste. Bake and put the layers together with White Mountain Cream.

Election Cake. Work with the hand, scant ½ cup butter into 1 cup bread dough; add 1 egg well beaten. 1 cup brown sugar and ½ cup milk; add ¾ cup raisins, stoned and cut into pieces. and 8 chopped figs. Mix and sift together 1½ cups flour, 1½ teaspoonfuls Rumford Yeast Powder. 1 teaspoonful salt. 1 teaspoonful cinnamon, ¼ teaspoonful clove, ¼ teaspoonful mace, ¼ teaspoonful nutmeg, and add to the first mixture. Turn into a well-buttered bread pan and let rise 1¼ hours. Bake in a slow oven 1 hour.

Coffee Cake. Cream ¼ cup butter, add gradually ½ cup sugar. Add ½ cup molasses, 2 eggs well beaten, ½ pound raisins stoned and cut into pieces, and ½ cup coffee. Mix and sift 2½ cups flour. 2½ teaspoonfuls Rumford Yeast Powder, ½ teaspoonful salt. ½ teaspoonful cinnamon, ½ teaspoonful allspice, ½ nutmeg grated, and add to the first mixture. Bake in a cake pan 50 minutes.

Rich Coffee Cake. Cream ½ cup butter, add gradually 1 cup sugar. Add 2 tablespoonfuls molasses, 2 eggs well beaten, ½ cup raisins, ½ cup currants, 2 tablespoonfuls citron, cut fine, and ½ cup coffee.' Mix and sift together 2 cups flour, 2 teaspoonfuls Rumford Yeast Powder, ½ teaspoonful salt, ½ teaspoonful cinnamon, ½ teaspoonful clove, and ¼ teaspoonful nutmeg, and add to the first mixture. Bake in a deep cake pan 1¼ hours.

Sponge Cake. Beat the yolks of 4 eggs until thick, add gradually 1 cup sugar; beat 2 minutes. Add 3 tablespoonfuls cold water. Mix and sift together 1½ tablespoonfuls cornstarch, 1 scant cup flour, 1 teaspoonful Rumford Yeast Powder and ¼ teaspoonful salt; add to the first mixture the whites of the eggs beaten stiff and 1 teaspoonful extract lemon. Bake in a buttered angel cake pan 45 minutes, or shallow cake pan 35 minutes in a moderate oven.

Snow Cake. Cream ¼ cup butter, add gradually 1 cup sugar and ½ teaspoonful vanilla. Beat the whites of 2 eggs to a stiff froth and add. Mix and sift 1½ cups flour and 1½ teaspoonfuls Rumford Yeast Powder; add to the first mixture alternately with ½ cup milk. Bake in a moderate oven 45 minutes. Cover with boiling frosting.

Lily Cake. Cream ¼ cup butter, add gradually 1 cup sugar, ½ teaspoonful lemon extract and ⅔ teaspoonful vanilla. Beat 3 egg whites to a stiff froth and add. Mix and sift 1¾ cups flour and 2½ teaspoonfuls Rumford Yeast Powder; add to first mixture alternately with ½ cup milk. Bake and cover with chocolate frosting.

Cream Almond Cake. Cream 1 cup butter, add gradually 2 cups sugar and ½ teaspoonful almond extract. Mix and sift 1 cup cornstarch, 2 cups flour and 2 teaspoonfuls Rumford Yeast Powder. Add alternately with 1 cup milk to the first mixture. Beat 5 egg whites until stiff; add and beat vigorously. This makes two loaves.

Wellesley Cake. Follow the recipe for Cream Almond Cake, omitting the almond. To one-third of the mixture add 1½ squares melted chocolate, and ½ teaspoonful cinnamon. Cover the bottom of the pan with the white mixture; add the chocolate mixture, and the remainder of the white mixture by tablespoonfuls, that the cake may have a marbled appearance.

Marshmallow Cake. Cream ½ cup butter, add gradually 1½ cups sugar and 1 teaspoonful vanilla. Beat the whites of 5 eggs to a stiff froth and add. Mix and sift 2½ cups flour and 2 teaspoonfuls Rumford Yeast Powder; add to the first mixture alternately with ½ cup milk. Bake in layers. Spread marsh-mallow paste between the layers and on top.

Fig Eclair. Mix together 1 scant cup butter, 2 cups sugar, 1 cup milk, 8 egg whites, 3¾ cups flour and 3½ teaspoonfuls Rumford Yeast Powder. Bake ½ the mixture in 2 layers. Spread fig filling between the layers and frost with White Mountain Cream.

NOTE:—For using remainder of mixture, see Prune Almond Cake.

Prune Almond Cake. Bake the remainder of the Fig Eclair mixture in layers. To the remainder of the White Mountain Cream add six soft prunes cut in pieces, and twelve almonds blanched and shredded. Spread between the layers.

Golden Orange Cake. Cream ¼ cup butter, add gradually ½ cup sugar, 1 teaspoonful orange extract and 5 egg yolks beaten until light-colored. Mix and sift scant cup flour and 1 teaspoonful Rumford Yeast Powder; Add alternately with ¼ cup milk to the first mixture. Bake in a narrow, deep cake pan.

Gold Loaf Cake. Cream ¼ cup butter, add gradually ¾ cup sugar and 4 egg yolks beaten until light-colored. Mix and sift 1 cup flour and 1 teaspoonful Rumford Yeast Powder; add alternately with ¼ cup milk to the first mixture. Bake in a narrow, deep cake pan.

Boston Favorite Cake. Cream ⅔ cup butter, add gradually 2 cups sugar and 4 well beaten eggs. Mix and sift 3½ cups flour and 3½ teaspoonfuls Rumford Yeast Powder; add alternately with 1 cup milk to the first mixture. Bake in square cake tins. This makes two loaves.

Velvet Cake. Cream ½ cup butter, add gradually 1½ cups sugar, 3 well-beaten egg yolks and ⅓ cup cold water. Mix and sift 1½ cups flour, 2 teaspoonfuls Rumford Yeast Powder, ½ cup cornstarch, and add with the beaten whites of 4 eggs. Cover with Opera Caramel Frosting.

Orange Cake. Cream ¼ cup butter, add gradually 1 cup sugar. Add 2 eggs well beaten, ½ cup milk, and 1¾ cups flour mixed and sifted with 1½ teaspoonfuls Rumford Yeast Powder. Bake in layers. Spread Orange Filling between the layers and Orange Frosting on top.

Lemon Filled Cake. Cream ½ cup butter, add gradually 1½ cups sugar, 4 well beaten egg yolks and ⅔ cup milk. Mix and sift 2¼ cups flour and 2 teaspoonfuls Rumford Yeast Powder and add. Add the egg whites beaten until stiff. Bake in layers and put together with Lemon Filling.

Cream Pie. Cream ⅓ cup butter, add gradually 1 cup sugar, 2 well beaten egg yolks and ½ cup milk. Mix and sift 1¾ cups flour and 2 teaspoonfuls Rumford Yeast Powder and add. Add the egg whites beaten until stiff. Bake in Washington pie tins. Fill with Cream Filling.

Cocoanut Pie. Mix and bake as Cream Pie, using Cocoanut Filling.

Chocolate Pie. Cream ¼ cup butter, add gradually 1½ cups sugar, 2 well beaten egg yolks and 1 cup milk. Mix and sift 2⅔ cups flour and 2½ teaspoonfuls Rumford Yeast Powder, add. Add the egg whites beaten until stiff. Bake in layers, using Chocolate Filling between the layers and on top.

FILLINGS.

Cream. Mix 1 cup sugar, ⅓ cup flour and 2 eggs well beaten. Stir into 2½ cups hot milk. Cook in top of a double boiler 10 minutes. Add 1 teaspoonful vanilla.

Lemon. Mix together 1 cup sugar, 2½ tablespoonfuls flour, 1 egg, 1 teaspoonful butter, the grated rind of 2 lemons, and the juice of 2 lemons. Cook, stirring constantly until the boiling point is reached.

Orange. Mix together ½ cup sugar, 1 egg, 1 heaping tablespoonful flour, 1 teaspoonful butter, the grated rind of ½ an orange, juice of ½ orange, and ½ tablespoonful lemon juice. Bring to a boil, stirring constantly; then cook in the top of a double boiler 10 minutes, so as to remove the raw taste of the flour.

Chocolate. Melt 3 squares chocolate; add ½ cup powdered sugar and 3 tablespoonfuls milk. Stir until smooth. Add ¼ cup powdered sugar and cook over hot water 20 minutes. Add ½ teaspoonful vanilla.

Marshmallow Paste. Boil together 6 minutes, ¾ cup sugar and ¼ cup milk. Melt ¼ pound marshmallows and add 2 tablespoonfuls hot water. Combine the two mixtures, add ½ teaspoonful vanilla and beat until stiff enough to spread.

Fig. Mix together ½ pound figs, chopped fine, ⅓ cup sugar, ¼ cup water and the juice of ½ lemon. Cook in the top of a double boiler until thick enough to spread.

Cocoanut. Beat the whites of 2 eggs until stiff; add enough powdered sugar to spread. Spread over the cake, and sprinkle with grated fresh cocoanut. Use for a layer cake, having the filling between and on top.

FROSTINGS.

Plain Boiled Icing. 1 cup granulated sugar, 6 tablespoonfuls boiling water; boil without stirring until the syrup will "thread" from a spoon. Beat the white of 1 egg stiff, and when syrup is done, pour while hot over the egg, beating rapidly until smooth and thick; flavor, and then pour over the cake. Some add a pinch of cream tartar.

Confectioner's. To 2 tablespoonfuls boiling water add enough confectioner's sugar to make the mixture the right consistency to spread. Add flavoring to please taste.

Gelatine. To ½ teaspoonful granulated gelatine add 2½ tablespoonfuls boiling water; when dissolved stir into it ¾ cup of confectioner's sugar and ½ teaspoonful vanilla. Beat until of the consistency to spread.

Milk. Boil 1½ cups sugar, ½ cup milk and 1 teaspoonful butter for 12 minutes. Remove from the stove, add ½ teaspoonful vanilla, (or other flavoring to taste,) and beat until of consistency to spread.

White Mountain Cream. Boil together 1 cup sugar and ⅓ cup water until it threads. Pour the syrup slowly into the beaten white of 1 egg. Beat until cool enough to spread. Add ½ teaspoonful vanilla, (or flavoring to taste.) One square of melted chocolate may be added for a delicious chocolate frosting.

Chocolate. Melt 2 squares chocolate. add ¾ cup sugar and 3 tablespoonfuls milk. Cook in the double boiler until smooth; add the yolk of 1 egg and cook 1 minute. Spread on the cake.

Caramel. Mix together 2 cups sugar, ½ cup milk and 1 teaspoonful butter. Place on the stove, and when the mixture begins to boil add 2 squares chocolate, melted. Boil 13 minutes. Remove from the stove, add ½ teaspoonful vanilla and beat until of the consistency to spread.

Opera Caramel. Cook 1½ cups brown sugar, ½ cup thin cream and ½ tablespoonful butter, until a ball is formed when the mixture is tried in cold water. Beat until ready to spread.

Orange. To the grated rind of 1 orange add 1 teaspoonful brandy, ½ teaspoonful lemon juice and 1 tablespoonful orange juice; let stand 15 minutes. Strain, add slowly the beaten yolk of 1 egg. Stir in confectioner's sugar to spread.

STEAMED PUDDINGS.

Fruit Roll. Into 1 quart sifted flour rub 2 tablespoonfuls shortening. Add 1 teaspoonful salt and 2 heaping teaspoonfuls Rumford Yeast Powder and mix with just enough milk to make a soft dough. Knead lightly, roll out on board about ¼ inch thick. Sprinkle thickly with sugar, dried currants, or currants and raisins mixed. Grate over this a little nutmeg, and add about ½ cup molasses. Roll up in a tight roll, pinch the dough up at either end so the fruit cannot escape, place on a well-buttered plate, put in steamer and steam about ½ hour. Serve with hard or a liquid sauce.

Steamed Apple Dumplings. Select nice cooking apples, as many as you wish dumplings; peel and core them. Make a dough the same as for Fruit Roll. Roll out on a board about ¼ inch thick, cut into pieces large enough to cover each apple. Put an apple in centre of each piece, fill space from which core was taken with sugar, sprinkled with a little clove or cinnamon; cover apple well with dough, place in well-buttered plate in steamer, and steam ½ hour. Serve as soon as removed from steamer.

Indian Meal Fruit Pudding. Mix 1 pint Indian meal, 1 pint wheat flour, 1 teaspoonful salt and 1 cup beef suet which has been finely chopped and freed from skin. Beat up 3 eggs, add to them 1 pint milk; add this to dry ingredients, then stir in 1 cup stoned raisins and ½ cup dried currants, well-floured, and 2 heaping teaspoonfuls Rumford Yeast Powder. Turn mixture into a well-greased pudding mould or tin pail, cover tightly and place in saucepan of boiling water, the water reaching about half way up the sides of mould. Boil for 3 hours. Serve with brandy sauce.

Steamed Cottage Pudding. Beat 3 eggs without separating, until light; add to them ½ cup sugar, 1 pint milk, 2 tablespoonfuls melted butter, ½ teaspoonful salt, 3½ cups flour and 2 heaping teaspoonfuls Rumford Yeast Powder. Turn into well-greased pudding mould, cover tightly, stand in saucepan of boiling water, the water reaching about half way up mould; cover the whole closely and boil 3 hours. Serve with wine sauce.

Soufflé au Oat. Beat thoroughly 2 eggs, 1 tablespoonful butter melted, 1 cup cold oatmeal, ½ pint milk, 1 cup flour and 1 heaping teaspoonful Rumford Yeast Powder. Turn into well-greased mould and boil 1 hour. Serve with liquid sauce.

Liquid Sauce. Beat 2 ounces butter, yolks of 3 eggs and ½ cup sugar together until light; add 1 gill boiling water; stir over fire an instant, then remove and add 2 tablespoonfuls brandy.

Rice Cabinet Pudding. Beat 3 eggs and ½ cup sugar together until light; add 1 cup milk, 2 cups flour, ½ teaspoonful salt, 1 tablespoonful butter melted, and 1 cup cold boiled rice. Beat vigorously; then add 1 cup raisins, seeded, and 1 cup currants well-floured. Sift and mix in thoroughly 2 teaspoonfuls Rumford Yeast Powder. Pour into a well-greased mould or tin pail; set in a boiler with sufficient boiling water to reach half way up the sides of mould; *steam constantly* for 3 hours. Serve hot with sauce. Do not allow the water in the boiler to stop boiling for a moment or the pudding will be heavy. Add *boiling* water if more is needed.

Light-Bread Dumplings. Pare, core and quarter enough tart apples to fill a two quart pudding dish more than half full; sprinkle well with sugar; add about ½ cup water. Cover with biscuit dough, patted out one inch thick and large enough to cover the apples. Place a tight-fitting cover over the dish, allowing the dough sufficient room to swell. Steam in a moderately quick oven for 1 hour. Serve while hot with sweetened cream flavored with nutmeg, or plum pudding sauce.

Cranberry Pluffs. To 1¼ cups stale bread crumbs rubbed very fine, add 1 cup milk, ½ cup sugar, 4 tablespoonfuls flour and 1 cup cranberry pulp; mix well; then sift in 1 teaspoonful Rumford Yeast Powder, and mix carefully with whites of 4 eggs beaten to a froth. Pour into well-buttered coffee or custard cups, filling half full; sprinkle with powdered sugar : set cups in steamer, or bake-pan half full of boiling water, cover closely and steam about 1 hour or less according to size. Serve with fruit pudding sauce.

Batter Pudding with Fruit. Sift with 2 cups flour, 2 teaspoonfuls Rumford Yeast Powder and ½ teaspoonful salt. Rub in cold 1 tablespoonful butter; beat 2 eggs light and add to flour with sufficient quantity of milk to make a very thick batter. Stir in as many cherries or raspberries and currants as you can, first dredging them with flour. Turn into well-buttered pudding mould or tin bucket, cover closely, place in a vessel of boiling water and steam continuously for 2½ hours. Serve with foamy sauce.

Christmas Plum Pudding. Chop very fine 1 pound candied orange and lemon peel, mixed; ½ pound citron, ½ ounce bitter almonds, 1 pound beef suet, having removed the skin and fibre; add 1 pound brown sugar, ½ pound bread crumbs, ½ pound flour, 1 pound cleaned currants, 1 pound sultanas, 1 pound layer raisins, stoned and soaked over night in 1 gill of brandy and 1 gill of orange and lemon juice, 1 teaspoonful salt, 1 nutmeg, grated, ¼ teaspoonful cloves and 1 teaspoonful cinnamon. Mix all very thoroughly together. Then add 8 eggs

Powder. Pack into well-buttered moulds or tin kettles. These
will keep a long time if boiled 8 hours when made, and 4 hours
longer when ready to use. Serve with hard or brandy sauce.

BAKED PUDDINGS.

New Portsdale Pudding. Pour 1 cup scalded flour over 1
cup fine *dry* bread crumbs; add 1 tablespoonful butter, cover
and soak for ½ hour; then add the well-beaten yolks of 2 eggs,
1 cup flour, ¼ cup sugar, a little salt, nutmeg and ginger to
taste, and grated rind of ½ lemon; beat well; then add ½ cup
currants, cleaned and floured, 1 heaping teaspoonful Rumford Yeast Powder and whites of eggs beaten to a froth; mix
carefully and pour into a buttered pudding dish. Bake in a
moderate oven 45 minutes. Serve hot from dish in which it is
baked.

Rumford Cottage Pudding. Beat together until light 1 cup
sugar, 2 ounces butter and yolks of 3 eggs; then add gradually,
stirring constantly, 1 cup cold water, then 3 cups flour; beat
hard; sift in 2 heaping teaspoonfuls Rumford Yeast Powder;
add whites of eggs beaten very light and mix carefully. Bake
in a well-greased cake tin in a moderate oven 45 minutes.
Serve hot with Lemon Sauce.

Plum Pudding. Cream 2 tablespoonfuls butter with ½ cup
sugar. Add to this 2 eggs well-beaten, 1 cup milk, 2 cups
flour and 1 cup very large raisins, seeded and well-floured.
Sift and stir in carefully 1 heaping teaspoonful Rumford Yeast
Powder. Turn into a well-greased cake pan and bake in a
moderately quick oven 45 minutes. Serve with hard sauce.

Huckleberry Pudding. Cream ⅔ of a cup of butter with 2
cups light brown sugar; add 1 cup milk and yolks of 4 eggs well-
beaten, about 3½ cups flour, enough to make a very stiff
batter, sifted with 2 heaping teaspoonfuls Rumford Yeast Powder. Now stir in 1 quart huckleberries and bake in a well-
greased pudding dish for 3-4 of an hour. Serve with liquid
sauce.

Baked Batter Pudding. Use recipe for Huckleberry Pudding; adding any small fruit in season.

Gem Peach Puddings. Sift well together 2 cups flour, ¼
teaspoonful salt and 1 heaping teaspoonful Rumford Yeast
Powder. Chop in 2 ounces butter; beat 2 eggs light and add
to ½ cup water; beat briskly and stir quickly into the flour,
making a very stiff batter; beat vigorously; then drop a spoonful of batter into each well-buttered gem pan, place on top half

a peach either fresh or canned; cover with another spoonful
batter and bake in a quick oven for 30 minutes. Serve hot with
sweetened cream. This quantity will make 8 little puddings.

German Apple Pudding.   Prepare a biscuit dough; roll
it out half an inch thick; place it in a biscuit pan, brush the top
well with butter or lard; cover entirely with even slices of
apples, arranged in symmetrical rows; dredge thickly with
sugar and add a little grated nutmeg. Cover closely with an
inverted pan or tin and bake in a quick oven 30 minutes. This
is nice made with peaches. Serve with cream.

RECIPES FOR THE CHAFING DISH.

*These recipes, although prepared especially for the use of
the Chafing Dish, will be equally satisfactory cooked over the
stove.*

Oyster Grill.   Wash, pick over and drain 1 pint of oysters.
Put in the chafing dish and cook until plump, removing the
liquor as it flows from the oysters. Season with butter, salt
and pepper, and serve at once with small crackers.

Celeried Oysters.   Wash 1 pint oysters, drain and dry between towels. Season with salt and pepper, dip in ½ cup melted
butter, then in ½ cup fine cracker crumbs, and cook in a hot
buttered chafing dish.   Arrange on four slices toast, pour over
1½ cups thin white sauce, and sprinkle with finely chopped
celery.

Oysters with Madeira.   Heat 1 pint oysters to the boiling
point, skim and drain. There should be ¾ cup oyster liquor.
Cook 2 tablespoonfuls butter and 2 tablespoonfuls mushrooms
5 minutes.   Add 2 tablespoonfuls flour and gradually the
oyster liquor, then the oysters, a few drops of onion juice, a few
grains of cayenne pepper, ½ teaspoonful salt, ½ teaspoonful
lemon juice, 1 egg yolk, and lastly 1 tablespoonful madeira
wine. Serve on 8 small square crackers.

Chicken and Oysters.   Melt 2 tablespoonfuls butter, add 3
tablespoonfuls flour, ½ teaspoonful salt, ½ saltspoonful celery
salt, ¼ saltspoonful pepper.   When well mixed add gradually
1 cup milk. Wash and drain 1 cup oysters and add them to
the first mixture with 1 cup cooked chicken, cut in dice. As
soon as the oysters are plump serve on five slices of toast.
Veal may be substituted for chicken.

Anchovy Toast with Egg.   Beat 5 eggs slightly, add ½
teaspoonful salt, ½ saltspoonful pepper and ½ cup milk. Melt 1
heaping tablespoonful butter, add the egg mixture and stir
until creamy. Spread 6 slices of toast with anchovy paste,
arrange on a platter and pour over the egg.

Eggs à la Goldenrod. Put 1 tablespoonful butter in chafing dish, and when bubbling add 1 tablespoonful flour, ½ teaspoonful salt, ¼ saltspoonful pepper and gradually ½ cup milk.   Add the whites of 3 hard boiled eggs, chopped fine. When hot pour over 3 slices of toast. Rub the yolks of eggs through a strainer over all and garnish with parsley.

Eggs with Cream. Melt 1 tablespoonful butter, add ¼ cup thin cream, and when hot add 4 eggs, breaking each egg in a cup and slipping into the chafing dish, care being taken not to break the yolks. Season with salt, pepper and cayenne to taste. When the whites are nearly firm sprinkle with cheese. Finish cooking and serve on four slices of toast.   This dish is better cooked over hot water.

Curried Eggs. Melt 2 tablespoonfuls butter, add 2 table-spoonfuls flour, ¼ teaspoonful salt, ½ teaspoonful curry powder, ¼ saltspoonful pepper; when well mixed add gradually 1 cup milk, and 3 hard boiled eggs cut in eighths lengthwise.

Cheese with Eggs. Soak ½ cup stale bread in 1 cup milk until soft.   Melt ½ tablespoonful butter, add ½ cup mild cheese, cut fine, and stir until the cheese is melted.   Add the bread and milk with 1 egg, beaten, and ½ teaspoonful salt and a few grains of cayenne. Cook 3 minutes; pour over six slices of toast and poach 3 eggs in hot water and use as a garnish.

Oyster Rarebit. Parboil 1 cup oysters and remove the tough muscle.   Drain and reserve the liquor.   Melt 2 table-spoonfuls butter, add ½ pound cheese, cut fine, and ¼ teaspoonful salt and a few grains of cayenne. Beat 2 eggs, add the oyster liquor, and add gradually to the melted cheese.   Then add the oysters and serve on toast.

Plain Rarebit. Melt 2 tablespoonfuls butter, add ½ pound cheese, cut fine, ¼ teaspoonful salt and a few grains of cayenne. When the cheese is nearly melted add gradually ½ cup thin cream, and 2 egg yolks, slightly beaten.   Then pour over 12 Zephyrettes, (crackers).

Buttered Lobster. Remove the meat from a 2 pound lobster and chop slightly.   Melt 3 tablespoonfuls butter, add the lobster, and salt, pepper, lemon juice to taste.   Serve as soon as thoroughly heated.

Lobster, Delmonico Style. Melt ¼ cup butter, add 2 tea-spoonfuls flour, ½ teaspoonful salt, a few grains cayenne, slight grating of nutmeg and 1 cup thin cream. When this has thick-ened add the meat from a 2 pound lobster, cut in ½ inch dice. When thoroughly heated add 2 raw egg yolks and a wine glass of sherry.

White Fish, à la Provencale. Melt 4 tablespoonfuls butter, add 3 tablespoonfuls flour, and when well mixed add 2 cups milk. Flake 1 pound cooked halibut, and add with 4 egg yolks, hard boiled, rubbed through a strainer and mixed with 1 teaspoonful anchovy essence.

Swordfish with Cucumber Sauce. Wipe 1 pound swordfish, ½ inch thick, and season with salt and pepper. Melt 1 tablespoonful butter and sauté the fish. cooking it, by turning frequently for 7 minutes, Grate 2 cucumbers and drain from their liquor. Season with salt, pepper and vinegar to suit the taste.

Chickens' Livers with Madeira Sauce. Cut 6 chickens' livers in halves, season with salt and pepper; dredge with flour and sauté in butter. Brown 2 tablespoonfuls butter, add 3 tablespoonfuls flour and 1 cup brown stock. Reheat the livers and add 2 tablespoouiuls sherry and serve.

Chickens' Livers with Bacon. Wipe and cut 2 chickens' livers into 6 pieces and season with salt and pepper. Wrap each piece of liver in a slice of bacon and fasten with a skewer. Cook in the chafing dish, turning often.

Mock Terrapin. Melt 3 tablespoonfuls butter, add 2 tablespoonfuls flour, ¼ teaspoonful salt, ¼ saltspoonful pepper, a few grains of cayenne, and gradually 1 cup milk. Add 1½ cups chicken or veal cut in dice, yolks of 2 hard boiled eggs chopped fine, whites cut in larger pieces. Cook 3 minutes, add 3 tablespoonfuls wine and serve.

Warmed over Mutton. Brown 2 tablespoonfuls butter, add 3 tablespoonfuls flour. ¼ teaspoonful salt. ¼ saltspoonful pepper. Cook 2 minutes, add 1 cup brown stock, and when thick beat up ¼ tumbler currant jelly and add. Heat 6 slices of mutton, (allow the meat to heat.) and add 1½ tablespoonfuls sherry. If mutton gravy be at hand, use instead of making brown sauce.

Breaded Tongue with Tomato Sauce. Cut 6 slices of cooked corned tongue a little less than ½ inch thick. Take ½ cup dried bread crumbs and 1 egg. Dip the prepared tongue in the egg crumbs and sauté in butter. Place on a dish and pour around the sauce. Cook ½ can tomatoes, 1 slice onion, a bit of bay leaf, 15 minutes; strain, and add 3 tablespoonfuls butter and 3 tablespoonfuls flour cooked together. Season to taste with salt and pepper.

Meat Balls. Chop ½ pound lean raw beef fine, using a meat chopper if you have one. Season to taste with salt, pepper and a few drops of onion juice. Make in small balls without packing the meat too closely, handling the meat as little as possible. When the chafing dish is hot, butter just enough to prevent sticking; toss in the balls, shake gently for 3 minutes and season with salt, pepper and butter.

Devilled Tomatoes. Remove the skins from 3 tomatoes, and cut each in 3 slices. Season with salt and pepper, dredge with flour and sauté in butter. Place on a dish and pour over the dressing. Cream 4 tablespoonfuls butter and add 2 teaspoonfuls powdered sugar, 1 teaspoonful mustard, ¼ teaspoonful salt, a few grains of cayenne, 1 egg yolk, hard boiled, rolled to a paste, 1 whole egg beaten slightly, and 2 tablespoonfuls vinegar; cook until it thickens.

Fried Apples. Wipe, core and cut 4 sour apples in ½ inch slices. Sprinkle with 3 tablespoonfuls powdered sugar and pour over 3 tablespoonfuls port wine. Let stand 30 minutes. Then fry, using enough butter to prevent sticking. Serve with venison or mutton.

Soufflés aux Rhum. Beat the yolks of 2 eggs until thick; add gradually 6 tablespoonfuls powdered sugar and continue beating. Beat whites of 4 eggs until stiff and dry, and fold into the mixture. Butter the pan, turn in half of the mixture, brown and fold. Be careful not to overcook. The centre should be soft and creamy. Flavor with 1 tablespoonful rum.

SALADS.

NOTE.—The materials and ingredients used in the making of salads should be thoroughly chilled. Salads should be kept in a cold place until serving time. If allowed to stand in a warm pantry the crisp greens become wilted.

Chicken Salad. Mix equal parts of cold boiled chicken cut in dice, and celery cut in small pieces. Season with French dressing, and chill. Moisten and garnish with mayonnaise, hard boiled egg yolks, and pickles.

Lobster Salad, No. 1. Season equal parts of lobster cut in half-inch dice, and celery cut in small pieces, with a French dressing. Serve on a bed of lettuce with mayonnaise, and garnish with curled celery.

Lobster Salad, No. 2. Prepare as Lobster Salad No. 1, omitting the celery. Garnish with lettuce leaves and the coral rubbed through a strainer.

Sweet Bread and Cucumber Salad. Cook a pair of sweet breads in boiling water, with one-half tablespoonful each of salt and vinegar. Drain, cool, and cut in half inch dice. Add an equal amount of cucumber dice, season with salt and pepper, and moisten with cream dressing. Arrange lettuce leaves in nests. Put a tablespoonful of salad in each. Garnish with dressing, cucumber pickles and capers. Allow a slice of pickle for the centre of each nest, surrounded by capers.

Oyster and Chicken Salad. Wash and parboil one pint oysters. Drain and chill. Mix with an equal amount of cold boiled chicken cut in dice. Add dressing to suit taste. Arrange on a platter, surrounded with lettuce leaves.

Egg Salad. Remove the yolks from six hard boiled eggs. Chop the whites fine. Arrange on lettuce leaves, in nest shapes. Place a yolk in the centre of each nest. Serve with French dressing.

Cabbage and Celery. Remove the centre from a small, firm, white cabbage. Cut very fine with a sharp knife. Keep in ice-water for one hour. Drain, and mix with equal parts of celery cut in small pieces. Add cream dressing, and refill the cabbage. Arrange on a folded napkin, and garnish with the tops of the celery.

Dressed Lettuce. Wash, drain and pick over a head of lettuce, discarding the outer leaves. Arrange in its original shape, and serve with French dressing.

Lettuce and Radish Salad. Prepare and arrange as for dressed lettuce. Wash, scrape and cut six radishes into thin slices. Place between the lettuce leaves, and garnish with round radishes, cut to represent tulips.

Lettuce and Cucumber Salad. Rub the inside of a salad-bowl with a clove of garlic, first dipped in salt. Wash and drain one head of lettuce, arrange in the bowl, and place between the leaves sliced cucumber. Serve with a French dressing.

Tomato and Lettuce Salad. Peel and chill four medium-sized tomatoes, cut in halves crosswise. Place each half on a lettuce leaf. Garnish with mayonnaise, pressed through a pastry bag.

String-Bean Salad. Season one quart cold, boiled string beans, cut into pieces, with French dressing. Add one-half tablespoonful of chives, cut very fine.

SALAD DRESSING.

Mayonnaise Dressing. Mash thoroughly 1 hard boiled egg yolk and add a few grains of cayenne, ½ teaspoonful salt. ½ teaspoonful mustard; then add 2 raw egg yolks.   To this add ¾ cup olive oil slowly, at first drop by drop; as it thickens thin slowly with vinegar until 2 tablespoonfuls are used.

Cream Dressing. Mix together thoroughly ½ tablespoonful salt, ¼ tablespoonful mustard, 2 tablespoonfuls sugar, 1 teaspoonful flour, 2 egg yolks, 2½ tablespoonfuls melted butter and ¾ cup cream.   Then add slowly ¼ cup vinegar.   Cook over hot water until it thickens.   Strain and chill.

French Dressing. Mix together 1 teaspoonful salt and ¼ teaspoonful pepper.   Then add 2 tablespoonfuls vinegar, 4 tablespoonfuls oil, and stir until well blended.

RECIPES FOR TEAS, RECEPTIONS, Etc.

In making beverages of hot water, the water should be freshly boiled,

Russian Tea. Scald the teapot, which should be of earthen or china.   Put in 3 teaspoonfuls tea and pour over 3 cups boiling water.   Let stand in a warm place to infuse 5 minutes. Serve with a slice of lemon to each cup, and loaf sugar to taste; or add lemon juice and sugar to taste, and garnish with candied cherries.

Iced Tea. Pour hot tea over crushed ice.

Coffee. Wash 1 egg, break and beat slightly.   Dilute with half a cup cold water, add the crushed shell and mix with 1 cup of ground coffee.   Turn into a scalded coffee pot, pour on 6 cups boiling water and boil for 3 minutes.   Stir thoroughly, add ¼ cup cold water and place on the back of the stove for 10 minutes.   Serve with sugar and cream.

Café Noir. Put 1 cup ground coffee into a filter.   Place the filter in a coffee pot and pour over 3½ cups boiling water.   As soon as it has filtered through it is ready to serve.   If desired stronger, refilter.   The most popular mixture is ⅔ Java and ⅓ Mocha.

Chocolate. Scald 3 cups milk; melt 1½ squares of chocolate in a saucepan placed over a tea kettle; add 4 level tablespoonfuls sugar, a few grains of salt, and gradually 1¼ cups boiling water. Stir until perfectly smooth. Place on the front of the stove and boil 1 minute.   Then add to the scalded milk, and beat with an egg-beater 2 minutes.   Serve in chocolate cups with or without whipped cream.

Cocoa. Scald 1 quart milk; mix 4 tablespoonfuls prepared cocoa and 4 level tablespoonfuls sugar, and add enough boiling water from 1 cup to form a thin paste, then add the remainder of the water and boil 1 minute. Pour into the scalded milk, and beat with an egg-beater 2 minutes. Serve in chocolate cups with whipped cream, sweetened and flavored with vanilla. This is not as rich as chocolate, and is a desirable substitute at 5 o'clock teas.

Pineapple Lemonade. Make a syrup by boiling 1 cup sugar and 1 pint water for 10 minutes. Then add 1 can grated pineapple and juice of 3 lemons. Cool, strain, and add 1 quart of ice-water. Serve in lemonade glasses.

Fruit Punch. Make a syrup by boiling 2 cups sugar and 1 cup water for 10 minutes. Add 1 cup tea, 1 pint strawberry syrup, juice of 5 lemons, juice of 5 oranges, 1 can grated pineapple. Let stand 30 minutes; strain, add enough ice-water to make 1½ gallons of liquid, turn into a large punch bowl over a piece of ice, and add ½ pint Maraschino Cherries, and 1 quart bottle of Apollinaris Water. This amount will serve 50 people.

Sandwiches. Sandwiches prepared from bread which must lie for several hours before serving, can be kept fresh and moist by wrapping in a napkin wrung out of hot water and put in a cool place. In preparing bread for sandwiches, cut as thin as possible, and if to be buttered, cream the butter before spreading, or butter the bread before cutting from the loaf. Remove crusts and cut in oblongs, triangles or fancy shapes.

Russian Sandwiches. Spread zephyrettes (crackers) with thin slices of cream cheese; cover with chopped olives mixed with mayonnaise. Place a zephyrette over each, and press together.

Chicken Sandwiches. Spread thin slices of bread cut in fancy shapes with cold boiled chicken mixed with mayonnaise. Serve on a doily.

Nut Sandwiches. Mix equal parts of grated Swiss cheese and chopped English walnut meat. Season with salt and cayenne. Spread between thin slices of bread, slightly buttered, and cut in fancy shapes.

Jelly Sandwiches. Spread thin slices of buttered bread with quince jelly. Sprinkle with chopped hickory-nut meat and cover with buttered bread.

Salted Almonds. Blanch half a pound of almonds by pouring over them 1 pint boiling water, and let stand 3 minutes. Drain and cover with cold water. Remove the skins and dry the almonds on a towel. Fry in hot fat, using equal parts of butter and lard. Drain on brown paper and sprinkle with salt.

www.ingramcontent.com/pod-product-compliance
Lightning Source LLC
Chambersburg PA
CBHW021437090426
42739CB00009B/1516